Joy to the World

Sacred Christmas Music
Through the Ages

ALBERT AND SHIRLEY MENENDEZ

CUMBERLAND HOUSE
NASHVILLE, TENNESSEE

For Barbara,
the musical one in the family

The authors would like to express their gratitude to Carl Daw Jr. of the Hymn Society in the United States and Canada, Boston University School of Theology; Mary Louise VanDyke of the Dictionary of American Hymnology, Oberlin College Library; and Bishop Payne of the Library, Virginia Theological Seminary.

Published by
CUMBERLAND HOUSE PUBLISHING, INC.
431 Harding Industrial Drive
Nashville, TN 37211
www.cumberlandhouse.com

Scripture quotations are from the King James Version of the Holy Bible.

Library of Congress Cataloging-in-Publication Data

Menendez, Albert J.
    Joy to the world : sacred Christmas songs throughout the ages / Albert J. Menendez and Shirley C. Menendez.
        p.   cm.
    Includes bibliographical references (p.) and index.
    ISBN 1-58182-205-7 (alk. paper)
    1. Christmas music—History and criticism. 2. Carols—History and criticism. 3. Hymns—History and criticism.
    I. Menendez, Shirley C., 1937–   . II. Title.
    ML2880.M46 2001
    782.28'0723—dc21   2001032547

Printed in the United States of America

1 2 3 4 5 6 7 8 9 10 — 05 04 03 02 01

CONTENTS

Introduction

More than a century ago, in 1862, Christopher Wordsworth, England's foremost Greek scholar and a bishop in the Church of England, wrote these moving words as part of a Christmas hymn:

Sing, O sing, this blessed morn,
Unto us a child is born,
Unto us a son is given,
God himself comes down from heaven;
Sing, O sing, this blessed morn,
Jesus Christ to-day is born.

To Bishop Wordsworth, nephew of the great poet William Wordsworth, Christmas was a time for singing, a time for putting religious thoughts and convictions into poetry and song. This sentiment was fairly common— after all, this was the era of Charles Dickens and the strolling carolers called "waits"—and it certainly was not new, for the previous fifteen centuries had seen the creation of many Christmas hymns, songs, and carols.

That remarkable tradition is the subject of this book: some of the great songs that best express the spiritual side of Christmas. While many other wonderful songs celebrate home and family, romance and winter, these songs express the underlying reality of the Christmas season from Advent until the Epiphany.

The songs selected are those we regard as the most enduring and permanent on the musical landscape, the ones that have stood the test of time and evoke a variety of moods and emotions associated with the fundamental meaning of Christmas.

These are the songs that appear most frequently in hymnals or on concert programs, services of lessons and carols, or that top the lists of favorite Christmas music. They reflect many different eras of history and different climes and cultures. The stories of their origins, the reasons why they were written, and why they have become so popular are explored.

There are, of course, many other songs, particularly in Latin America, Asia, Africa, and Eastern Europe, that have not yet attained widespread popularity in the United States and Western Europe. Perhaps at some future date they will be as popular as those included in this book. And we have included some less well-known songs that seem to us to speak eloquently of Christmastide.

Please note that many of these songs have been published in multiple versions and translations through the years; thus, lyrics may differ slightly from the version with which you are most familiar. Also, some of the songs were written in one country, while the music came from another. We placed them in the section we thought most appropriate.

We hope this book will enrich your celebration of Christmas as you enjoy the music of the season.

I

AMERICAN, CANADIAN, AND CARIBBEAN SONGS AND HYMNS

American religious Christmas music has a long and surprising history, the more so because for many years Christmas was celebrated only in some religious communities. Episcopalians, Catholics, Lutherans, the Reformed Dutch and German Churches, and Moravians celebrated Christmas with worship services and with the inherited traditions of their respective European cultures. But Baptists, Methodists, Presbyterians, Quakers, and Evangelicals did not observe the holiday at all.

As late as 1857, the *New York Times* reported that "yesterday Christmas services were held in Catholic, Episcopal, and Lutheran churches, where evergreen and music were plentiful. The churches of the other denominations were closed." But a half century later a "devotional revolution" had taken place in the Sunday schools, and churches of just about every tradition had set aside historical and theological objections to celebrating Christmas. This trend intensified throughout the twentieth century, and churches of different faith traditions began to share each other's liturgies and best-loved hymns and carols. They also drew upon the common and shared cultural heritage of Christmas music that developed outside the formal structures of the church.

This section includes a few American Christmas carols and hymns. Many more were included in our previous work, *Christmas Songs Made in America*. William Billings, a New Englander from a religious tradition that frowned on Christmas, may have been the first composer of an American Christmas hymn (see "A Virgin Unspotted," page 34).

The American Moravians who settled in Bethlehem, Pennsylvania, and Winston Salem, North Carolina, were noted for their love of music and for their contributions to the realm of Christmas music. A movement that began in Central Europe in the fifteenth century, the Moravians were part of the Reformed Protestant tradition; and they preserved many of the customs, traditions, holy days, and church musical traditions of the Catholic tradition, and added their own contributions as well.

The Moravians celebrated Christmas with a rich, profound, and prayerful liturgy. The great Moravian Christmas carol "The Morning Star" was written in 1836 by a minister, Francis F. Hagen. Hagen acknowledged in later life that music was the great love of his life, more than pastoring. This carol, often sung by a child, expresses the ancient sentiment comparing Jesus to light that shines in darkness, or in this case, a morning star that is brighter than the sunshine. The word *Jesulein* can best be translated as "christ child."

"THE MORNING STAR"

Morning Star in darkest night,
Strikes the earth with joyful light;
Jesulein,
Come be mine,
Fill my heart with light divine.

Thine own sparkling splendor bright,
Far excels the sun's great light;
Thou alone
Jesulein

Art a thousand suns sublime.
Now, oh come, my soul's true Light,
Come be mine, dispel my night,
Come be mine,
Jesulein,
Fill my heart with light divine.

Another Moravian anthem, "How Beautiful upon the Mountains," is "comparable to the finest choruses of Haydn and Mozart," says James S. Darling, organist and choirmaster of Bruton Parish Church in Williamsburg, Virginia. Its author, John Antes, was born in Bethlehem in 1740 but served as a Moravian missionary in Egypt and eventually settled in England. The simplicity of this carol is evident in its opening verse (from Isaiah 52:7): "How beautiful upon the mountains are the feet of him that bringeth good tidings, that publisheth peace; that saith unto Zion, thy God reigneth."

A stirring choral anthem for Christmastide, "Sing, O Ye Heavens," was written by Johann Friedrich Peter. Born in Holland, Peter immigrated to Bethlehem, Pennsylvania, in 1770 and lived at various times in North Carolina, Maryland, and New Jersey before his death in 1813. He wrote nearly a hundred anthems for worship. The words to "Sing, O Ye Heavens" are joyous.

> *Sing, O ye heavens! The Savior is here!*
> *Rejoice all ye nations! The Savior is here!*
> *Shout ye with gladness! The Savior is here!*
> *God lies in a manger, in flesh now appearing.*
> *In Him is joy; in Him is eternal life.*
> *Praise Him, ye Christians, with jubilant singing.*
> *God, our Redeemer, our Savior is here.*
> *Sing with the angels, sing hallelujah!*
> *Glory be to Thee, praise and hallelujah!*

German Lutheran immigrants to Pennsylvania contributed "Away in a Manger" to our repertory of Christmas music. African-American spirituals also include a few Christmas songs, primarily focusing on the domestic scenes of the Nativity.

The "Negro Spirituals" are a uniquely American contribution to musical history, arising as they did among slaves on the plantations of the Old South. They are music from the heart, born of the experience of suffering. Arising spontaneously in a circumscribed culture, these songs often admit to no authorship. As in other folk cultures, they were part of oral tradition and belonged to the community in which they arose. Now they belong to the world.

The best-loved African-American spirituals for Christmas include "Go Tell It on the Mountain," "Mary Had a Baby," and "Rise Up, Shepherd, and Follow," which are included in *Christmas Songs Made in America*. In this chapter we include "The Virgin Mary Had a Baby Boy," an Afro-Caribbean song that originated in Trinidad.

Spirituals of Appalachian origin are also a part of the American musical landscape. "As Joseph Was A-Walking" and "I Wonder As I Wander" are splendid examples of this musical idiom that appeared in our first volume.

Two early examples of Scotch-Irish flavor may be cited here. "The Babe of Bethlehem" speaks in the highly stylized language of the eighteenth and early nineteenth centuries.

"THE BABE OF BETHLEHEM"

To Abraham the promise came, and to his seed forever,
A light to shine in Isaac's line, by Scripture we discover;
So hail the morn, the Savior's born, the glorious Mediator;
God's blessed Word made flesh and blood, assured
the human nature.

His parents poor in earthly store, to entertain the stranger,
They found no bed to lay His head, but in the ox's manger.
No royal things, as used by kings, were seen by those
who found Him,
But in the hay the stranger lay with swaddling
bands around Him.

The city's name is Bethlehem, in which God hath appointed,
This glorious morn a Savior's born, for Him God hath anointed.
By this you'll know, if you will go, to see this little stranger;
His lovely charms in Mary's arms, both lying in a manger.

Another example from the Shenandoah Valley of Virginia called "Hither Ye Faithful" is simpler in construction.

"HITHER YE FAITHFUL"

Hither ye faithful,
Haste with songs of triumph,
To Bethlehem go, your Lord of Life to meet,
To you this day is born a Prince and Savior
O come and let us worship at His feet.

Shout his almighty name,
Ye choirs of angels,
And let the celestial courts His praise repeat;
Unto our God be Glory in the highest
O come and let us worship at His feet.

American religious music for the Christmas season was enhanced by the works of Alfred Burt, a minister's son from the Upper Peninsula of Michigan who became a New York and Hollywood star before his untimely death in 1954. Burt never forgot his religious upbringing, and he composed many sacred songs, such as "Sleep, Baby Mine" and "Some Children See Him."

Several examples of the American Christmas music tradition are included in this section.

"Away in a Manger"

This familiar carol has long been popular, especially with children. Its tender, simple verses are so personal in nature that those who sing or hum along to the carol feel transported back to Bethlehem. A lullaby, it is meant to be sung to a baby or young child. Jesus is addressed as Lord, and He is depicted as sleeping on hay with "no crib for a bed."

The third stanza suggests that the baby Jesus does not cry much, which may be wishful thinking or poetic fancy on the part of the author! The fifth and sixth stanzas change character somewhat, addressing Jesus in heaven and pleading with Him to stay close to the petitioner and to bless all children.

The lullaby has been a rich part of religious poetry and of Christian folklore and music. Robert Herrick's "The Burning Babe" may be the most literate example of the form. A fifteenth-century carol from Chester, England, "Lully Lully La" is an early example of the lullaby, as is the Czech carol "Jesus Dear, Sleep in Peace."

Many people will be surprised to learn that "Away in a Manger" is American in origin and was not written by Martin Luther in the sixteenth century. The musical scholars who prepared the *Companion to the Hymnal: A Handbook to the 1964 Methodist Hymnal* wrote: "All that can be said confidently about the origin of this carol is that Martin Luther himself had nothing to do with it. The evidence suggests that it is wholly an American product. The original form probably originated among German Lutherans in Pennsylvania about 1885."

This is an example of how an inaccuracy is compounded through the years. Anonymous verses entitled "Away in a Manger" appeared in 1885 in a book called *Little Children's Book for Schools and Family* published in Philadelphia by the Evangelical Lutheran Church in North America. In 1887 "Away in a Manger" appeared again in James Ramsey Murray's *Dainty Songs for Little Lads and Lasses*, which called this "Luther's Cradle Hymn." Since the initials JRM appear in the upper right corner, Murray evidently wrote the music for this lullaby. Why he chose to perpetuate the ruse of Luther as the author of the lyrics is a mystery. Perhaps he wanted to capitalize on the Luther name since Luther was enormously popular in nineteenth-century America, and 1883 had been the four-hundredth anniversary of Luther's birth.

The myth was repeated until a brilliant work refuting it was written by Richard S. Hill in the "Music Library Association Notes" in December 1945. Through painstaking and exhaustive research, Hill concluded that there was no German original of "Away in a Manger" in Luther's voluminous writings, which had been published and translated for more than four centuries. None of Luther's many biographies had ever alluded to such a work, even though Luther wrote many carols, including the well-known "Von Himmel Hoch" (From Heaven on High I Come).

There are many musical settings, all written by Americans. *The Hymnal Companion 1940* (Episcopal) noted, "By 1891 the carol was sweeping the country, largely due to Murray's repeated publication of his setting. During 1891 four new musical settings appeared, with three more in the

following year." *The Episcopal Hymnal* uses an 1895 tune by William Kirkpatrick. Some other church hymnals prefer J. B. Herbert's 1891 version. Others prefer a tune written by Jonathan Spilman.

Even today, more than fifty years after its origins were definitively established, song books still refer to this as Luther's cradle hymn.

"Away in a Manger"

Away in a manger,
No crib for a bed,
The little Lord Jesus
Laid down His sweet head.

The stars in the sky
Looked down where He lay,
The little Lord Jesus,
Asleep on the hay.

The cattle are lowing,
The Baby awakes,
But little Lord Jesus,
No crying He makes.

I love Thee, Lord Jesus,
Look down from the sky,
And stay by my cradle
Till morning is nigh.

Be near me, Lord Jesus,
I ask Thee to stay,
Close by me forever,
And love me, I pray.

Bless all the dear children
In Thy tender care
And take us to heaven,
To live with Thee there.

"It Came Upon the Midnight Clear"

Born in 1810 in the village of Sandisfield in the Berkshire Hills of western Massachusetts, Edmund Hamilton Sears was one of those quiet men whose lives are measured in the enduring calm of plains and meadows, as opposed to peaks and valleys. One of his ancestors was among the original Pilgrims who settled in Plymouth in the early seventeenth century.

Except for his college years at Union College in Schenectady, New York, Sears spent his entire life in small Massachusetts towns. After briefly studying law, he changed career plans and entered Harvard Divinity School, graduating in 1837. He was ordained to the Unitarian ministry and held four pastorates during his lifetime. It is said he had no ambition to pastor large or influential city churches but was content as a rural parson.

Sears wrote a number of religious books and coedited a religious magazine. He rarely traveled, but a trip to England in 1873 was a signal delight. He was well known in his denominational circles and drew large crowds to his sermons.

Nineteenth-century New England Unitarians were much more conservative than their brethren would be a century later, and Sears wrote frequently about his belief in the divinity of Christ. It may be of some interest that two other Unitarian hymn writers of that century were Sarah Flower Adams, author of "Nearer, My God, to Thee," and Sir John Bowring, who wrote "In the Cross of Christ I Glory."

Sears is best remembered today for his lovely carol "It Came Upon the Midnight Clear," written in 1849 and first appearing in the magazine *Christian Register.* The *Christian Register's* editor, a fellow clergyman, wrote some time later, "I always feel that, however poor my Christmas sermon may be, the reading and singing of this hymn are enough to make up for all deficiencies."

This carol shows the author's skillful use of poetry and imagery, as in "harps of gold," "the world in solemn stillness lay," and a reference to God as "heaven's all-gracious King." The second stanza is highly descriptive of the angelic choir, while the third and fifth stanzas take on an almost political tone, with descriptions and intimations of a future golden age of peace. Those who suffer injustice are encouraged to "hear the angels sing." This emphasis on angels explains why this carol was often called "The Blessed Angels Sing."

The music for Sears's poem was written by Richard Storrs Willis, a journalist and musician born in 1819. Willis was a Yale graduate who lived in New York, edited the *Musical World* magazine, and wrote books on church music and related subjects. He studied music in Germany, where the great composer Felix Mendelssohn was one of his teachers. After he returned to New York, he became a music critic for the *New York Tribune*. While a member of the vestry at the Episcopal Church of the Transfiguration (better known as "The Little Church Around the Corner"), Willis wrote the music to "It Came Upon the Midnight Clear."

Interestingly, Sears wrote an earlier Christmas carol when he was just twenty-four years old. Entitled "Calm on the List'ning Ear of Night," it was published in the *Boston Observer* in 1835 and was praised by Oliver Wendell Holmes as "one of the finest and most beautiful ever written." The lines bear a good measure of similarity to his more famous carol. It reads:

"CALM ON THE LIST'NING EAR OF NIGHT"

Calm on the list'ning ear of night
Come heaven's melodious strains,
Where wild Judea stretches forth
Her silver-mantled plains;
Celestial choirs from courts above
Shed sacred glories there;
And angels, with their sparkling lyres,
Make music on the air.

The answering hills of Palestine
Send back the glad reply,
And greet from all their holy heights
The Dayspring from on high:
O'er the blue depths of Galilee
There comes a holier calm;

And Sharon waves in solemn praise
Her silent groves of palm.

"Glory to God!" the lofty strain
The realm of ether fills;
How sweeps the song of solemn joy
O'er Judah's sacred hills!
"Glory to God!" the sounding skies
Loud with their anthems ring:
"Peace on the earth; good will to men,"
From heaven's eternal King.

This day shall Christian tongues be mute,
And Christian hearts be cold?
O catch the anthem that from heaven
O'er Judah's mountains rolled,
When burst upon that listening night
The high and solemn lay,
"Glory to God; on earth be peace":
Salvation comes today.

This early carol was set to music by John Edgar Gould, a composer and author of eight books of religious and secular songs. Gould, who died in Algiers in 1875, wrote the music for the sailor's hymn "Savior, Pilot Me."

Sears lived out his life as a country pastor. He died in January 1876 at the age of sixty-five. While his books are forgotten, his carol "It Came Upon the Midnight Clear" is still sung and admired a century and a half after it appeared. In fact, the eminent scholar Alfred Edward Bailey, writing in his 1950 classic *The Gospel in Hymns*, made this observation: "No Christmas is perfect without the singing of this hymn. It is one of the finest ever written, not only because of its melodious rendering of the Biblical story of angels and shepherds, but because it is one of the first to emphasize the social significance of the angels' message."

"IT CAME UPON THE MIDNIGHT CLEAR"

It came upon the midnight clear,
That glorious song of old,
From angels bending near the earth,
To touch their harps of gold;
"Peace on the earth, good will to men,
From heaven's all gracious King";
The world in solemn stillness lay
To hear the angels sing.

Still through the cloven skies they come
With peaceful wings unfurled,
And still their heavenly music floats
O'er all the weary world;
Above its sad and lowly plains
They bend on hovering wing,
And ever o'er its Babel sounds
The blessed angels sing.

Yet with the woes of sin and strife
The world hath suffered long;
Beneath the angel-strain had rolled
Two thousand years of wrong;

And man, at war with man, hears not
The love song which they bring:
O hush the noise, ye men of strife,
And hear the angels sing.

O ye, beneath life's crushing load,
Whose forms are bending low,
Who toil along the climbing way
With painful steps and slow;
Look now! for glad and golden hours
Come swiftly on the wing;
O rest beside the weary road,
And hear the angels sing!

For lo! the days are hastening on
By prophet-bards foretold,
When with the ever-circling years
Comes round the Age of Gold;
When peace shall over all the earth
Its ancient splendors fling,
And the whole world send back the song
Which now the angels sing.

"Jesus, Jesus, Rest Your Head"

The eminent Kentucky folklorist and collector of authentic folk songs John Jacob Niles included a number of Christmas songs in his collections of folk music in Appalachia and the Southern Highlands. Niles adapted and harmonized the music, but the lyrics likely span several generations of oral transcription.

We probably will never know who wrote the words to these Christmas songs. We are not even certain that they originated in the mountainous regions of the southeastern United States. They may have come from the British Isles to the U.S. during the waves of immigration of the eighteenth and nineteenth centuries. But then again, their style and language suggest possible Appalachian origins.

John Jacob Niles was born in Louisville on April 28, 1892, and his father taught him the ballads and songs of eastern Kentucky's mountainous region. Young John also learned how to make dulcimers, a lovely instrument often used in the folk-music culture of the region.

Niles was a World War I veteran who studied music in France after the war and at the Cincinnati Conservatory of Music. He spent many years collecting and annotating folk songs, ballads, and carols of Appalachia, and published a number of books containing his discoveries. *Life* magazine did a full-scale portrait of Niles in the September 6, 1943, issue, hailing him as an authentic folksinger and preserver of a unique American music idiom. He was called "the minstrel of Boone Creek"; his work is truly an American achievement.

In *Christmas Songs Made in America* we told the story of "I Wonder As I Wander," one of the most moving and haunting Christmas songs ever produced. Niles discovered this gem while visiting Murphy, North Carolina, a small town in Cherokee County. At a revival meeting of some itinerant evangelists (who were being kicked out of town by the mayor!), Niles heard the song intoned by a young girl named Annie Morgen. He paid her a quarter to repeat the verses for him so he could preserve them for future generations. He never encountered her again, nor would he ever find a trace of this song in any existing collection of carols.

"Jesus, Jesus, Rest Your Head" is a fine example of the cradlesong, or lullaby. The cradlesong focuses tenderly on the baby Jesus and the humble surroundings of His birth. These poetic verses show the humanity of Jesus, especially in His helpless newborn state when He was totally dependent on His mother for warmth, sustenance, and protection.

Niles said he "adapted" this from "the singing of three people in Hardin County, Kentucky," sometime in the early 1930s. The simplicity of the language suggests a very rural origin, with phrases like "You has got a manger bed" and "His mammy went to that stable on that Christmas Eve so late." Cows were said to be "lowing" and even "milkmaids left their fields and flocks." There is a good deal of poetic imagination in this charming little lullaby. The wise men did not bring gifts, but "things from hin and yon for the mother and the father and the blessed little Son."

A decided preference toward the underdog is expressed in this song since "all the evil folk on earth sleep in feathers at their birth." Jesus, of course, is one of us, the authors of this song imply, since He is born in rural poverty and has only a manger in which to rest His head.

The unknown author of this song links the birth of little Jesus to His destiny in a cryptic phrase, "Have you heard about our Jesus? Have you heard about His fate?" Niles dedicated his translation and adaptation to his five-year-old son, Thomas.

Cradlesongs have a long heritage in Christmas music. They are found in all the European countries, and Germany, Austria, Central Europe, and the Slavic nations have produced some of the most notable. An endearing Polish lullaby, "Infant Holy, Infant Lowly," has found its way into many hymnals. A Czech carol, "Jesus, Dear, Sleep in Peace, and Do Not Fear" is popular in that region of Europe.

In America, "Away in a Manger," which originated among the German Lutheran communities in Pennsylvania during the 1880s, has long been a favorite carol. Sung in Sunday schools, church pageants, and in worship services, it remains a standard in the Christmas repertory (see page 7).

John Jacob Niles's research in Appalachia uncovered some other wonderful Christmas songs, such as "Sweet Little Jesus Boy" and "The Carol of the Birds."

"JESUS, JESUS, REST YOUR HEAD"

Have you heard about our Jesus?
Have you heard about His fate?
How His mammy went to that stable
On that Christmas Eve so late?
Winds were blowing, cows were lowing,
Stars were glowing, glowing, glowing.

Refrain:

Jesus, Jesus, rest Your head,
You has got a manger bed.
All the evil folk on earth
Sleep in feathers at their birth.
Jesus, Jesus, rest Your head,
You has got a manger bed.

To that manger came then wise men,
Bringing things from hin and yon.
For the mother and the father
And the blessed little Son.
Milkmaids left their fields and flocks
And sat beside the ass and ox.

"O Little Town of Bethlehem"

The first two lines of "O Little Town of Bethlehem" convey a message of peace and tranquillity, and a sense of the eternal. The contrast between "dark streets" and "the everlasting light" immediately catches our attention.

A sense of history and author Phillips Brooks's belief in the incarnation of the Son of God are conveyed in the fourth line of the first stanza, which refers to "the hopes and fears of all the years" being caught up or "met" in the birth of Christ. All five stanzas are rich in history, symbolism, and a kind of tenderhearted theology that appeals to people of all ages.

It is perhaps unsurprising that its author was a man of the cloth whose sermons were so well received that they often became public events in nineteenth-century America. Brooks was Boston-born and Harvard-educated. He had, as was often remarked, good prospects for a successful life, owing to the advantages of his childhood, but it took a while for young Brooks to find his niche. As a professor of Latin in the famed Boston Latin School, which he had attended as a youth for five years, he was a failure. The ministry suited him best. It was his destiny.

Brooks had always been a scholarly young man, graduating third in his class at Boston Latin and entering Harvard at the age of sixteen. He left Boston in October 1856 for the Virginia Theological Seminary to prepare for the Episcopal priesthood and was ordained in 1859, spending the next ten years at two Philadelphia parishes, the Church of the Advent and the Church of the Holy Trinity, the latter a prominent parish on fashionable Rittenhouse Square.

Brooks's forte was preaching, and people were attracted to his sermons by his eloquence and sincerity. He took a special interest in ministering to Union soldiers during the Civil War, and he called President Abraham Lincoln's Emancipation Proclamation "the greatest and most glorious thing our land has ever seen."

It was during his days at Holy Trinity that "O Little Town of Bethlehem" was born. Brooks was physically exhausted from his strenuous activity during the war years, and Holy Trinity granted him a year's leave of absence with full salary from July 1865 to July 1866. He spent most of it in Europe, arriving in the Holy Land just before the Christmas of 1865. He and his party rode on horseback for the two-hour journey to Bethlehem. The little town left an indelible impression on his memory, as did a five-hour worship service at the Church of the Nativity, which is traditionally said to be on the very spot of the holy birth. Brooks kept a detailed diary of his experiences

It has long been argued that Brooks did not write "O Little Town" until three years later in Philadelphia, but that may be an error perpetuated by numerous writers. Brooks's noted biographer, church historian Raymond W. Albright, wrote, "It is now almost certain that Brooks wrote his hymn 'O Little Town of Bethlehem' that night in or near those fields in Bethlehem, just as on other occasions when deeply moved he wrote his best poetry." An early biographer, A. V. G. Allen, also asserts this in his many-volumed *Life and Letters of Phillips Brooks*, published in 1900 and 1901. Allen interviewed a companion on the journey who told him that Brooks had written the poem "on the spot," something Brooks appeared to have corroborated in a letter to Lucy Larcom (a popular novelist of the day) dated December 28, 1886.

Whenever it was written, the poem became a hymn in a rather extraordinary way. Brooks had customarily prepared an original carol for the Christmas services at his parish Sunday school class. In 1868, he gave a copy of "O Little Town" to his organist, Lewis H. Redner, and asked Redner to write the music. Redner, a businessman and Sunday school superintendent, could not find the time or inspiration for the task. As Christmas approached, he had still not written a line of music. Then something quite unexpected occurred. Writes Raymond Albright: "Redner had little success in preparing an appropriate tune until the night before rehearsal when he was 'roused from sleep late in the night hearing an angel strain whispering in my ear.' He jotted down at once the melody and the next morning before church filled in the harmony. The children at Holy Trinity learned it eagerly and sang it regularly each Christmastide, but it was to be at least a decade until the well loved hymn was widely known and sung."

In later years, Brooks was a bit bemused by the lavish attention given to "O Little Town." In a letter to author Lucy Larcom, he confessed, "It has been printed in hymn books and sung at a good many Christmases. Where the newspapers found it all of a sudden I do not know."

This was the last Christmas for Brooks in Philadelphia, as he was called to be rector of the old and historic Trinity Church in Boston in 1869. Brooks, who never married, became nationally celebrated for his sermons at Trinity until his death at the age of fifty-seven in 1893.

Brooks was so admired that the day of his funeral, January 26, 1893, was designated an official day of mourning in Massachusetts. Stores were closed, as was the stock exchange. Thousands passed by his bier at Trinity Church on Copley Square. His honorary pallbearers included President Charles Eliot of Harvard University, Justice Horace Gray of the United States Supreme Court, and best-selling novelist Weir Mitchell. The presiding bishop of the Episcopal Church officiated at the service, and long lines of mourners greeted his funeral cortege as it made its way to Mt. Auburn Cemetery across the Charles River in Cambridge.

Brooks was devoted to Christmas as a festival of the church. He wrote numerous Christmas poems and carols, including "Christmas Once Is Christmas Still." His "Christmas Sermon" received national acclaim in *Century* magazine in December 1893. A decade after Brooks's death, his book *Christmas Songs and Easter Carols* was published. An essay, "A Constant Christmas," appeared in 1890.

Brooks wrote two other carols that were once popular. In 1961 Christmas historian Daniel Foley claimed that "everyone who loves Christmas knows a few lines of 'Everywhere, Everywhere, Christmas Tonight,'" a poem-carol by Brooks. It celebrates the universality of the Christmas message with such lines as:

> *For the Christ-child who comes is the Master of all,*
> *No place too great and no cottage too small;*
> *The angels who welcome Him sing from the height,*
> *In the City of David a King in His might.*

In "The Voice of the Christ-Child" Brooks became more reflective and meditative. He reminds his listeners that the child of Bethlehem came for "the sad and the lonely, the wretched and poor," offering hope to those who "dared not dream of it before." His opening stanza sings out, "The earth has grown old with its burden of care, but at Christmas it always is young." And he closes with these thoughts:

> *The feet of the humblest may walk in the field*
> *Where the feet of the holiest have trod,*
> *This, this is the marvel to mortals revealed,*

When the silvery trumpets of Christmas have pealed,
That mankind are the children of God.

His lovely recollection of that first Christmas in Bethlehem is no longer just enjoyed by one Sunday school class in Philadelphia, but by people all over the world. On the centennial of its first appearance, the *Christian Century*, editorialized that "O Little Town" will live forever because it is "a carol which is perfect in its simplicity and wonder."

"O LITTLE TOWN OF BETHLEHEM"

O little town of Bethlehem,
How still we see thee lie!
Above thy deep and dreamless sleep
The silent stars go by;
Yet in thy dark streets shineth
The everlasting Light;
The hopes and fears of all the years
Are met in thee tonight.

For Christ is born of Mary,
And gathered all above,
While mortals sleep, the angels keep
Their watch of wondering love.
O morning stars, together
Proclaim the holy birth,
And praises sing to God the King,
And peace to men on earth!

How silently, how silently,
The wondrous Gift is given!
So God imparts to human hearts
The blessings of His heaven.
No ear may hear His coming,
But in this world of sin,
Where meek souls will receive Him, still
The dear Christ enters in.

Where children pure and happy
Pray to the blessed Child,
Where misery cries out to Thee,
Son of the mother mild;
Where charity stands watching
And faith holds wide the door,
The dark night wakes, the glory breaks,
And Christmas comes once more.

O holy Child of Bethlehem,
Descend to us, we pray;
Cast out our sin, and enter in,
Be born in us today.
We hear the Christmas angels
The great glad tidings tell;
O come to us, abide with us,
Our Lord Immanuel!

"Shout the Glad Tidings"

President Andrew Jackson loved this unusual Christmas hymn of early nineteenth-century America. It is unusual because it does not mention the Nativity; it retells the Song of Miriam in Exodus 15:21. But its author, William Augustus Muhlenberg, rector of Trinity Church in New York, thought the sentiments could be applied to Jesus at His coming. Muhlenberg wrote that he composed the hymn "at the particular request of Bishop Hobart," the Episcopal bishop of New York, "who liked the verses I made so well that he had them struck off before the hymns were published and sung in Trinity Church on Christmas Day." It was added to the Episcopal hymnal of 1826 but was dropped in the revision of 1982.

William Augustus Muhlenberg was born in Philadelphia in 1796, the great-grandson of the patriarch of the Lutheran Church in America, Henry Melchior Muhlenberg. William, however, soon began to attend Christ Episcopal Church, a church associated with many of the signers of the Declaration of Independence and an institution in Philadelphia life.

Eventually he became a priest in the Episcopal Church. But he remembered with fondness the Lutheran hymns of his early youth and tried to stimulate a richer hymn-singing tradition in his new denomination. In 1824 he wrote, "A Plea for Christian Hymns," since the American Episcopal Church of that time authorized only fifty-seven hymns for the entire year of worship. Two years later his church's General Convention authorized the preparation of an official hymnbook, and Muhlenberg was asked to join the committee selecting the hymns. Another member was Maryland lawyer Francis Scott Key, author of "The Star-Spangled Banner."

Muhlenberg and his colleagues created a popular volume of hymnody. He contributed four original hymns of his own to the collection, including "Shout the Glad Tidings," which became a Christmas favorite even though it was not directly about the Nativity.

Muhlenberg never married; but he loved children, and his baptismal hymn, "Saviour, Who Thy Flock Art Leading," was widely sung. He became head of a boys' school in New York City and rector of the Church of the Holy Communion. He also founded St. Luke's Hospital.

On his deathbed at well past his eightieth year, Muhlenberg had a lighthearted disagreement with the hospital chaplain. Muhlenberg told the chaplain, "You are asking God to restore me, and I am asking God to take me home. There must not be a contradiction in our prayers, for it is evident that He cannot answer them both." Muhlenberg's prayer was answered, and he slipped quietly into eternity.

"SHOUT THE GLAD TIDINGS"

Zion, the marvelous story be telling,
The Son of the Highest, how lowly His birth!
The brightest archangel in glory excelling,
He stoops to redeem thee, He reigns upon earth.

Refrain:
Shout the glad tidings, exultingly sing,
Jerusalem triumphs, Messiah is King!

Tell how He cometh; from nation to nation
The heart-cheering news let the earth echo round:

How free to the faithful He offers salvation,
His people with joy everlasting are crowned.

Mortals, your homage be gratefully bringing,
And sweet let the gladsome hosanna arise:
Ye angels, the full alleluia be singing;
One chorus resound through the earth and the skies.

"'Twas in the Moon of Wintertime"

This is the oldest carol written in North America. It was penned in the early seventeenth century by a French missionary priest, Father Jean de Brebeuf. Brebeuf, who was descended from William the Conqueror and Saint Louis, King of France, was born in 1593 in the Normandy region of the country. He became a priest and teacher in the old cathedral town of Rouen (painted so beautifully centuries later by Claude Monet).

In 1626 he was sent as a missionary to New France, as Quebec was then called. He worked among the Huron Indians, where he both earned their respect and interacted favorably with them. After returning briefly to France, he returned to his Huron converts in 1633. Unfortunately, goodwill toward the French missionaries had evaporated, and rivalries between the Iroquois and Huron peoples had intensified. As a result, Brebeuf and a number of his fellow missionaries were put to death on March 16, 1649. His followers scattered, but, somehow, some Huron converts to Christianity preserved this Huron-language carol.

A century later, another French Jesuit missionary, Etienne de Villeneuve, prepared a manuscript of Brebeuf's

lyrics and translated them into French. Villeneuve was
pastor of the descendants of the Huron Christians who
had survived the massacre of 1649. Villeneuve and Paul
Piccard translated many of the Huron hymns and chants
into French and preserved their original language versions
in writing. Until then they had been handed down orally
from generation to generation.

Still, the carol had received no attention outside of
rural Quebec until 1899 when a Toronto-based journalist
and choir director, Jesse Edgar Middleton, discovered it in
a French-language volume of old carols from Quebec.
Middleton did his own translation into English, and the
carol achieved recognition and a new life. His freewheeling
translation, beginning with the haunting phrase, "'Twas in

the moon of wintertime when all the birds had fled," is generally the one used today. Some older song books called it "The Huron Carol" or "Jesus Is Born." A sixteenth-century French folk song became the melody.

In an attempt to convey the meaning of the first Christmas to his converts, Brebeuf had written this carol using Huron settings and language. The wise men became "chiefs," and the gifts of the Magi became "fox and beaver pelt." The shepherds became "hunters," and the swaddling clothes were transformed into "a ragged robe of rabbit skin." This unusual carol is at once the oldest North American carol and one of the newest admitted to many denominational hymnals, such as those of the Lutheran, Presbyterian, Roman Catholic, and Episcopalian churches.

Canonized as saints by Pope Pius XI in 1930, Brebeuf and his fellow missionaries were later proclaimed Canada's patron saints. Today they are remembered by a shrine near their place of martyrdom in Quebec. They are also remembered in Upstate New York at the "shrine of the North American martyrs."

"'TWAS IN THE MOON OF WINTERTIME"

'Twas in the moon of wintertime
When all the birds had fled,
That mighty Gitchi Manitou
Sent angel choirs instead.
Before their light the stars grew dim,
And wandering hunters heard the hymn:

Refrain:
Jesus, your King, is born.
Jesus is born.
In excelsis gloria!

Within a lodge of broken bark
The tender Babe was found,
A ragged robe of rabbit skin
Enwrapped His beauty round.
And as the hunter braves drew nigh,
The angel song rang loud and high:

The earliest moon of winter time
Is not so round and fair,
As was the ring of glory
On the helpless Infant there.
While chiefs from far before Him knelt,
With gifts of fox and beaver pelt.

O Children of the forest free,
O sons of Manitou,
The Holy Child of earth and heav'n
Is born today for you.
Come, kneel before the radiant Boy
Who brings you beauty, peace, and joy.

"The Virgin Mary Had a Baby Boy"

This Calypso-flavored folk tune probably originated in Trinidad. Folklorist Edric Conner relates that he first heard this song when he was in Trinidad in 1942. A ninety-four-

year-old man, James Bryce, who still worked on a grape-
fruit plantation, sang the lyrics for Conner. Bryce had
learned it from his parents and grandparents.

The syntax and rhythm have clear echoes of Africa,
and this Afro-Caribbean spiritual has become a popular
Christmas song since it was introduced to Americans and
Europeans a half century ago.

"The Virgin Mary Had a Baby Boy"

The Virgin Mary had a baby boy,
The Virgin Mary had a baby boy,
The Virgin Mary had a baby boy,
And they say that His name was Jesus.

Refrain:
He come from the glory,
He come from the glorious kingdom;
He come from the glory,
He come from the glorious kingdom;
Oh, yes! Believer;
Oh, yes! Believer;
He come from the glory,
He come from the glorious kingdom.

The angels sang when the baby born,
The angels sang when the baby born,
The angels sang when the baby born,
And proclaim Him the Savior Jesus.

The wise men saw when the baby born,
The wise men saw when the baby born,

The wise men saw when the baby born,
And they say that His name was Jesus.

"A Virgin Unspotted"

William Billings, a colonial "Yankee tunesmith," may have written the first American Christmas hymn. Born in Boston in 1746, Billings was a tanner's apprentice who taught himself music. He taught music in churches and schools and was a prolific composer of original hymns, not mere paraphrases of psalms. Thus, Billings "marks the beginning of modernity in church songs in America," according to the authoritative *Oxford Companion to Music*.

What makes his Christmas music noteworthy is that very few Protestant churches in his native New England even celebrated Christmas as a religious or secular holiday during his lifetime. Christmas was not a legal holiday in Massachusetts until after the Civil War, and businesses and schools were open as usual on that day. Billings apparently felt the need to express his convictions that Christmas should be celebrated, as it had been for fourteen centuries in other cultures.

Billings was a patriot. He composed "Lamentation over Boston" when British troops occupied his hometown during the War of Independence. Sadly, he died in poverty on September 26, 1800.

Billings wrote several Christmas songs celebrating the role of the shepherds. One of them goes like this:

Shepherds rejoice, lift up your eyes,
And send your fears away;
News from the region of the skies,
Salvation's born today.

Jesus, the God whom angels fear,
Comes down to dwell with you;
Today He makes His entrance here,
But not as monarchs do.

Thus Gabriel sang, and straight around
The heavenly armies throng,
They tune their harps to lofty sound,
And thus conclude the song:

Glory to God that reigns above,
Let peace surround the earth;
Mortals shall know their Maker's love
At their Redeemer's birth.

Billings also composed "A Virgin Unspotted." This tune is anchored in its wonderful refrain, "Then let us be merry, put sorrow away, our Savior Christ Jesus was born on this day." This refrain, which follows each of the eight verses, is sung a little faster than the rest of the piece. It is a delightfully simple retelling of the Nativity story from Luke, with an unusual reference to "Adam's transgression" in the opening verse. It has a dancelike character but a precision of words that conveys the message in unmistakable conviction.

"A VIRGIN UNSPOTTED"

A virgin unspotted ye prophet foretold,
Should bring forth a Savior which now we behold;
To be our redeemer from death, hell and sin,
Which Adam's transgression involved us in.

Refrain:
Then let us be merry, put sorrow away,
Our Savior Christ Jesus was born on this day.

To Bethlehem, city of David, they came,
Both Joseph and Mary, to answer by name
The census of taxes which all had to pay,
For Caesar commanded it done on that day.

But when they had entered the city so fair,
A number of people so mighty was there
That Joseph and Mary, whose substance was small,
Could find in the inn there no lodging at all.

Then were they constrained in a stable to lie,
Where horses and oxen they used for to tie;
Their lodging so simple they took it no scorn,
But ere the next morning our Savior was born.

The King of all kings to this world being brought,
Small store of fine linen to wrap Him was sought;
But when she had swaddled her young son for sleep,
'Twas naught but a manger she laid Him to keep.

Then God sent an angel from heaven so high,
To certain poor shepherds in fields where they lie;
And bade them no longer in sorrow to stay,

Because that our Savior was born on this day.

Then presently after the shepherds did spy
Vast numbers of angels to stand in the sky;
They joyfully talked and sweetly did sing,
To God be all Glory, our heavenly King.

To teach us humility all this was done,
And learn we from thence haughty pride for to shun;
A manger His cradle who came from above,
The great God of mercy, of peace, and of love.

II

ENGLISH AND IRISH
SONGS AND HYMNS

English Christmas music is varied and plentiful. Carols, which originated as a kind of dance music, flowered in England as nowhere else, especially from about 1400 to 1550. The church frowned on the singing of carols, regarding them as too frivolous and insufficiently spiritual. Church councils banned them at times from the seventh century to as late as 1435.

When St. Francis of Assisi and his followers reinvigorated the customs of the Nativity crèche, they included songs in the celebrations. Ian Bradley, journalist, author, and minister of the Church of Scotland, noted, "It was almost certainly through Franciscans that Christmas carols came to the British Isles." Carols were popular in home settings and in festivals, and eventually they were brought into the church's liturgy, he says.

While the Reformation curbed the singing of carols and the Puritans tried to stamp out all Christmas observances, the love of carols did not die. In 1619 Lancelot Andrewes, the bishop of Winchester and one of the great theologians in a group called the "Caroline Divines," extolled Christmas as a day celebrated "as well at home with carols as in the church with anthems."

Carols slowly regained their popularity after the Puritan Cromwell dictatorship was overthrown. A few were sung in churches, and by the eighteenth century Oliver Goldsmith's novel *The Vicar of Wakefield* noted that churchgoers "kept up the Christmas carol." A century later Thomas Hardy's novel *Under the Greenwood Tree* lamented the passing of carolers in the English countryside.

For a century or more, a popular English custom was that of wandering bands of singers, called "waits," who went from house to house singing carols and begging refreshments or small stipends of money. These traditions merged with the wassailers, who went door-to-door singing and drinking to the health of the occupants.

During the nineteenth century, groups of musicians, scholars, and antiquarians, and even a few lawyers and politicians, began to research England's ancient carols and published their findings in book-length collections. This revival went hand in hand with Charles Dickens's celebration of Christmas in the secular world and with the Oxford Movement's struggle to restore hymns and carols to the worship of the Church of England. As Ian Bradley writes, "Carols played an important role in the Victorian re-invention of Christmas as a largely domestic festival full of sentimentality and good cheer. A huge number of new carols were written in the mid-nineteenth century, many in a pseudo-traditional style." Carol services soon spread to cathedrals, parish churches in remote areas, and college chapels. And many new carols saw the light of day in the twentieth century.

In this section we tell the stories behind some of the great carols from the English and Irish traditions.

"Angels from the Realms of Glory"

This lovely hymn first appeared as a Christmas Eve poem in an English newspaper in 1816, not long after Napoleon's defeat at the Battle of Waterloo and the ending of a second war between England and the United States. Its author was the paper's editor, James Montgomery.

Montgomery had edited *The Sheffield Iris,* an outspoken journal of opinion in a working-class town, for more than twenty years when he turned more to spiritual interests and began writing poems and hymns. He was a talented writer whose support of many unpopular causes, including foreign missions and the abolition of slavery, had landed him in jail. There was limited freedom of the press in the England of his day.

Montgomery overcame considerable hardship in his youth. His parents were Moravian missionaries to the West Indies who placed their six-year-old son in an austere boarding school. When they were killed, young James found himself mostly unwanted and neglected. He turned to poetry as solace, but his youth was a bitter catalog of homelessness, inadequate education, and despair. Soon he became a low-level employee at the newspaper he eventually purchased and edited. His passionate advocacy of the underdog and his stirring editorials made him a popular and valued member of the Sheffield community.

Meditating on the Christmas story for a Christmas Eve feature, Montgomery wrote this hymn, with its stately retelling of the angels and shepherds, and its refrain, calling for worship and recognition of the "newborn King." Its three remaining stanzas were aimed at "sages, saints, and sinners."

After it was published in book form in 1825, the poem was set to music by Henry Smart, a blind musician and composer. It appeared in a psalm and hymnbook designed for the worshipers at London's Regent Square Presbyterian Church. Hence the tune is often called "Regent Square" in hymnals.

In 1821 Montgomery wrote another stirring hymn, "Hail to the Lord's Anointed," which was introduced to a Moravian congregation on Christmas Day. Though based on the Seventy-second Psalm, it refers to the coming of "great David's greater son" and was often sung at Advent or Christmas services. Reflecting Montgomery's beliefs about social justice, it says that Jesus "comes to break oppression, to set the captive free" and that He comes especially "to those who suffer wrong to help the poor and needy and bid the weak be strong." Today it is often sung at ordinations. Montgomery was quite eclectic religiously, worshiping among the Moravians, Methodists, and Quakers.

Montgomery was so respected that he was granted a royal pension in his later years. The homeless boy also bought a mansion called "The Mount" on the highest point in Sheffield, where he was honored as "the first citizen" of the city. He wrote more than four hundred hymns. "Angels from the Realms of Glory" remains his Christmas masterpiece.

"ANGELS FROM THE REALMS OF GLORY"

Angels from the realms of glory,
Wing your flight o'er all the earth;
Ye, who sang creation's story,
Now proclaim Messiah's birth:

Refrain:
Come and worship, come and worship
Worship Christ, the new-born King.

Shepherds in the field abiding,
Watching o'er your flocks by night,
God with man is now residing;
Yonder shines the infant Light:

Sages, leave your contemplations;
Brighter visions beam afar:
Seek the great Desire of nations;
Ye have seen His natal star:

Saints before the altar bending,
Watching long in hope and fear,
Suddenly the Lord, descending,
In His temple shall appear:

"As with Gladness, Men of Old"

William Chatterton Dix was an unlikely author of hymns, spending most of his professional life selling insurance. The son of a prominent surgeon in Bristol, England, young Dix was born in 1837, the same year in which Queen Victoria ascended to the throne and Samuel F. B. Morse invented the telegraph.

Having no desire to follow in his father's footsteps, Dix moved to Glasgow, Scotland, and entered the insurance business. But as he suffered from serious and prolonged illnesses, he was often confined to his bed. While recuperating, he wrote a volume of poetry, *Hymns of Love and Joy,* and began to translate Greek and Ethiopian hymns into English, surely an unusual way to pass the time! He told his vicar, "There are some excellent hymns in the languages of both of those people."

Dix, who was "an obedient and dutiful High Churchman" in the Anglican tradition, according to one authority, took a considerable interest in worship and in studying the Bible. While meditating on the Scripture (Matthew 2:1–12) appointed for Epiphany in 1859, Dix felt moved to offer his view of the visit of the Magi. The result was this lovely, meditative hymn, sung on Epiphany as well as during the entire Christmas season. Dix wanted to penetrate to the heart of the mystery. He thus refers to "men of old" rather than Magi or wise men.

At the end of each stanza he urged his listeners to respond to the message of the "gracious Lord, our heavenly King." The fourth and fifth stanzas look to the future, where "ransomed souls" may enter into a "heavenly country" where no clouds hide the glory of our King.

Dix wrote the words to another beloved Christmas song, "What Child Is This?" discussed later in this volume.

"AS WITH GLADNESS, MEN OF OLD"

As with gladness, men of old
Did the guiding star behold;
As with joy they hailed its light,
Leading onward, beaming bright;
So, most gracious Lord, may we
Evermore be led to Thee.

As with joyful steps they sped
To that lowly manger-bed;
There to bend the knee before
Him whom heaven and earth adore;
So may we with willing feet
Ever seek the mercy-seat.

As they offered gifts most rare
At that manger rude and bare;
So may we with holy joy,
Pure and free from sin's alloy,
All our costliest treasures bring,
Christ! To Thee, our heavenly King.

Holy Jesus! Every day
Keep us in the narrow way;
And, when earthly things are past,
Bring our ransomed souls at last

Where they need no star to guide,
Where no clouds Thy glory hide.

In the heavenly country bright,
Need they no created light;
Thou its light, its joy, its crown,
Thou its sun which goes not down:
There forever may we sing
Alleluias to our King.

"Brightest and Best of the Sons of the Morning"

This Epiphany carol with a rather lengthy title was written by Reginald Heber in 1811 when he was the vicar of
a parish in the village of Hodnet, in Shropshire, England.
After receiving Holy Orders in the Church of England in
1807, Heber was also elected a fellow of All Souls College, reflecting his scholarly bent.

Heber wrote this carol on the spur of the moment
when he wrote the words in his daughter's school composition book. Its imagery is lush and almost mystical.
(Who are "the sons of the morning"?) The repetition in
the first and fifth stanzas of "Star of the east, the horizon
adorning, guide where our infant Redeemer is laid" is
quite felicitous. The second stanza is an evocative depic-
tion of the Nativity, in which the tiny child is hailed as
"Maker and Monarch and Saviour of all." The references
to "morning stars" and "son of God" may be allusions to
Job 38:7. Author and priest George Rutler says this song

"sings a piety of shimmering beauty." He adds, "All Epiphany is summed here: haunting, majestic, poignant, and ethereal and domestic."

Heber belonged to the evangelical wing of the Church of England but was devoted to a proper appreciation of church holy days and festivals, for which he wrote numerous poems and hymns. Though born wealthy, he was devoted to the care of the poor, which is reflected in the fourth verse, "Richer by far is the heart's adoration, dearer to God are the prayers of the poor."

Named the bishop of Calcutta, India, at the age of forty, Heber set off on a grand journey to a fabled land. His popular hymn "From Greenland's Icy Mountains" is often called the greatest missionary hymn of the nineteenth century. His style in that hymn, as in his others, was called "florid, fluent and picturesque" by an admirer. Heber died suddenly three years after arriving in India.

After his death, his wife, Amelia, gathered his poems and hymns in a book called *Hymns Written and Adapted to the Weekly Service of the Church Year.* His original manuscripts were donated to the British Museum, and he has been honored by Washington's National Cathedral.

In *Christ and the Carols,* William J. Reynolds contends that Heber was a "pioneer" in hymnody. He writes, "His hymns reveal a literary quality not found in his predecessors'. In earlier years theological content, doctrinal soundness, and scriptural accuracy were of prime concern. Now, poetic beauty emerges as a major factor in Christian song."

Heber is also remembered for "Holy, Holy, Holy," written for Trinity Sunday, the eighth Sunday after Easter. It is used in many denominational traditions.

"BRIGHTEST AND BEST OF THE SONS OF THE MORNING"

Brightest and best of the sons of the morning,
Dawn on our darkness, and lend us thine aid:
Star of the east, the horizon adorning,
Guide where our infant Redeemer is laid.

Cold on His cradle the dew-drops are shining,
Low lies His head with the beasts of the stall;
Angels adore Him in slumber reclining,
Maker and Monarch and Savior of all.

Shall we then yield Him, in costly devotion,
Odors of Edom, and offerings divine,
Gems of the mountain, and pearls of the ocean;
Myrrh from the forest, and gold from the mine?

Vainly we offer each ample oblation,
Vainly with gifts would His favor secure;
Richer by far is the heart's adoration,
Dearer to God are the prayers of the poor.

Brightest and best of the sons of the morning,
Dawn on our darkness, and lend us thine aid:
Star of the east, the horizon adorning,
Guide where our infant Redeemer is laid.

"Christians Awake, Salute the Happy Morn"

This may be the only Christian hymn that was composed at the request of the writer's daughter and presented to her, complete with red ribbon, on Christmas morning, probably in 1749.

John Byrom, the author, was born near Manchester, England, in 1692 and educated at Trinity College, Cambridge. He studied medicine in France but decided not to become a doctor. Upon his return to England in 1718, he invented a system of shorthand that was officially endorsed by an act of Parliament in 1742. Among his friends and pupils were John and Charles Wesley, who utilized his shorthand to write their copious journals, letters, hymns, and poems.

Byrom held some controversial political views, aligning himself with the Jacobites, or "nonjurors," who believed that William and Mary's "Glorious Revolution" of 1688 was illicit. The Jacobites, strongest in Scotland, supported King James II, a Catholic who was deposed and defeated by the Williamite forces largely because of his religion. Generally, High-Church Anglicans and Roman Catholics filled the ranks of the Jacobites, as did others who believed in the "divine right of kings." Bonnie Prince Charlie's rebellion had just failed a short time before Byrom composed this hymn. Byrom was influenced by a variety of religions, however, including Methodism and Quakerism, though he remained a member of the Church of England until his death in 1763.

In 1749 he promised his daughter, Dolly, that he would write a special Christmas poem for her. When she came to the breakfast table, she found an envelope addressed "Christmas Day, for Dolly." This beautiful poem, originally of 481 lines, was the result. Dolly was thrilled.

The first four stanzas retell the story of the Nativity from Luke. The second half bids the listener to remember and "ponder in our mind God's wondrous love in saving lost mankind."

After its publication in the *Manchester Mercury,* a local musician and organist of the parish church wrote the music to transpose a heartfelt poem into a hymn. He sent a copy to Byrom, and the two men became lifelong friends.

The following year, 1750, Byrom's diary records that "the singing men and boys, with Mr. Wainwright, came here and sang 'Christians Awake.'" The choir stood outside their window on Christmas morning and serenaded the composer and his Dolly.

For more than 250 years this serenely confident hymn for Christmas morning has delighted young and old alike. It appeared in the classic hymnal *Hymns Ancient and Modern* in 1860 and the *Episcopal Hymnal* in 1874. It now appears in song books of many Christian traditions.

"Christians Awake, Salute the Happy Morn"

Christians, awake, salute the happy morn,
Whereon the Savior of the world was born;
Rise to adore the mystery of love,
Which hosts of angels chanted from above;

With them the joyful tidings first begun
Of God incarnate and the Virgin's Son.

Then to the watchful shepherds it was told,
Who heard the angelic herald's voice: "Behold,
I bring good tidings of a Savior's birth
To you and all the nations on the earth:
This day hath God fulfilled His promised word,
This day is born a Savior, Christ the Lord"

He spake, and straightway the celestial choir
In hymns of joy, unknown before, conspire;
The praises of redeeming love they sang,
And heaven's whole orb with alleluias rang;
God's highest glory was their anthem still,
Peace on the earth, and unto men good will.

To Bethlehem straight the happy shepherds ran,
To see the wonder God had wrought for man;
And found, with Joseph and the blessed maid,
Her Son, the Savior, in a manger laid;
Amazed, the wondrous story they proclaim,
The earliest heralds of the Savior's name.

Let us, like these good shepherds, then employ
Our grateful voices to proclaim the joy;
Trace we the Babe, who hath retrieved our loss,
From His poor manger to His bitter cross;
Treading His steps, assisted by His grace,
Till man's first heavenly state again takes place.

Then may we hope, the angelic thrones among,
To sing, redeemed, a glad triumphal song;
He that was born upon this joyful day
Around us all His glory shall display;
Saved by His love, incessant we shall sing
Eternal praise to heaven's Almighty King.

"Come, Thou Long-Expected Jesus"

"Come, Thou Long-Expected Jesus" is a classic Advent hymn, a hymn of expectancy and longing for the fulfillment of age-old prophecies. It has often been hymn number one in hymnals that follow the church year.

Charles Wesley wrote this hymn for his *Hymns for the Nativity of Our Lord* in 1744. It took more than a century to gain acceptance, though, being added to the Methodist hymnal in 1875 and Episcopal hymnals in 1871, for example.

The music comes from an eighteenth-century German composer, Christian Friedrich Witt.

As is true with all of Wesley's extraordinary hymns, this one is sincere and forthright in language and style, and easily adaptable to congregational singing. Wesley used some traditional Advent imagery, referring to Jesus as the "hope of all the earth" and the "desire of every nation." A nice Christmas touch is found in the phrase "born a child, and yet a King."

"COME, THOU LONG-EXPECTED JESUS"

Come, Thou long-expected Jesus,
Born to set Thy people free;
From our fears and sins release us,
Let us find our rest in Thee.

Israel's strength and consolation,
Hope of all the earth Thou art;
Dear desire of every nation,
Joy of every longing heart.

Born Thy people to deliver,
Born a child, and yet a King,
Born to reign in us forever,
Now Thy gracious kingdom bring.

By Thine own eternal Spirit
Rule in all our hearts alone:
By Thine all-sufficient merit
Raise us to Thy glorious throne.

"God Rest Ye Merry, Gentlemen"

"God Rest Ye Merry, Gentlemen" is a kind of ballad or folk song. Written very much in the language and syntax of eighteenth-century England, it sounds very ancient, even antique, to modern listeners. Some scholars believe it to be even older, perhaps dating to the sixteenth century.

The song celebrates the birth of Jesus in a manger and uses the word *blessed* in reference to the Babe and to

His mother. The stanza celebrating the shepherds' arrival is a bit quaint, saying that "the shepherds rejoiced much in mind, and left their flocks-a-feeding." They also came "in tempest, storm and wind," which is an additional bit of information not recorded by St. Luke. The last stanza changes direction all together, by wishing "a merry Christmas" to "the ruler of this house," suggesting perhaps that this ballad was sung by strolling singers to serenade the lord of an ancient manor.

While jaunty and happy in style, the song is meant to convey religious teachings. A "blessed angel" "brought tidings" that the little baby born in Bethlehem was no other than "the Son of God by name." Twice the carol refers to the infant "savior" who came "to save us all from Satan's power when we were gone astray" and to "free all those who trust in Him from Satan's power and might."

"God Rest Ye Merry, Gentlemen" is a plea that "God may keep you in good spirits," according to Henry Simon. Part of the charm of this carol is its old-fashioned language, which would undoubtedly suffer if updated.

Fans of Charles Dickens's *A Christmas Carol* will remember that Scrooge heard the opening lines of this song and threatened the carolers with a ruler, since Scrooge hated Christmas and could not bear the thought of being happy.

Musical versions of *A Christmas Carol* always include "God Rest Ye Merry, Gentlemen," because of its association with the Dickens classic.

"GOD REST YE MERRY, GENTLEMEN"

God rest ye merry, gentlemen,
Let nothing you dismay,
Remember Christ our Savior
Was born on Christmas Day;
To save us all from Satan's power
When we were gone astray.

Refrain:
O tidings of comfort and joy,
Comfort and joy;
O tidings of comfort and joy!

From God our heavenly Father
A blessed angel came;
And unto certain shepherds
Brought tidings of the same;
How that in Bethlehem was born
The Son of God by name.

"Fear not, then," said the angel,
"Let nothing you affright;
This day is born a Savior
Of a pure Virgin bright,
To free all those who trust in Him
From Satan's power and might."

The shepherds at those tidings
Rejoiced much in mind,
And left their flocks a-feeding,

In tempest, storm and wind,
And went to Bethlehem straightway
This blessed Babe to find.

But when to Bethlehem they came,
Whereat this Infant lay,
They found Him in a manger,
Where oxen feed on hay;
His mother Mary kneeling,
Unto the Lord did pray.

Now to the Lord sing praises,
All you within this place,
And with true love and brotherhood
Each other now embrace;
This holy tide of Christmas
All others doth deface.

God bless the ruler of this house,
And send him long to reign,
And many a merry Christmas
May live to see again;
Among your friends and kindred
That live both far and near—
And God send you a happy new year, happy new year,
And God send you a happy new year.

"Good King Wenceslas"

This is the only song in this collection that does not mention the events surrounding the birth of Christ. Rather, it extols the good deeds of a Christian ruler on the day after Christmas in long-ago Bohemia! Still, it conveys the practical application of the teachings of the One whose birth is celebrated, and its proximity to Christmas places it within the twelve-day season traditionally associated with the Nativity.

"Good King Wenceslas" is based on the charitable acts and good works of a real-life ruler in early ninth-century Bohemia, a Central European kingdom now part of the Czech Republic. Despite his brief life span of twenty-four years or less, Wenceslas was noted for his generosity of spirit. His primary biographer wrote, "He was the honor of the clergy, the joy of the poor, the father of orphans, the defender of widows, the visitor of prisoners, the liberator of captives and the pious consoler of all in need. For in the heart of the blessed man, there burned the glorious fire of charity."

As with all hagiographies, the story of Wenceslas may have been embellished by retelling, and some of the basic facts may also be enshrouded in mystery. But it is certain that Wenceslas was a convert to the new Christian faith that was brought to Eastern Europe in the ninth century by two missionary brothers, Cyril and Methodius, who have been canonized by both the Roman Catholic and Eastern Orthodox Communions. Wenceslas had been converted under the influence of his grandmother Ludmilla, but his mother, Dragomir, despised Christianity and had her own mother strangled by assassins on September 16, 921.

Wenceslas took his Christian faith seriously, and "his acts of kindness became legendary throughout his kingdom even though his rule was a brief one," wrote Ernest K. Emurian. But his mother plotted her son's death and convinced her younger son, Boleslav, to kill his elder brother. The deed was accomplished on September 28, 935, when Boleslav hacked his brother to death with a hatchet at the door of the Church of Alt-Bunzlau. As he lay dying, Wenceslas said, "Brother, may God forgive you."

But Boleslav was haunted by the deed, and three years later he repented and reburied his brother in the Church of St. Vitus in Prague. Wenceslas's grave became a place of pilgrimage. Wenceslas the Holy was canonized, his feast day being September 28.

The carol recounts the king's custom of doing many charitable acts on the day after Christmas, which is also St. Stephen's Day, the day honoring the first Christian martyr. The linking of the two has made this a Christmas carol. The carol was written by John Mason Neale, an important figure in the history of Christmas music. Neale was both a translator and a writer of Christmas music as well as a scholarly priest in the Church of England in the nineteenth century.

John Mason Neale apparently uncovered the story of Wenceslas in an ancient collection of folklore and legends published in Sweden in 1582 and called the *Piae Cantiones.* When the British ambassador to Sweden came upon a copy in the National Museum in Stockholm and shared his findings with Neale, Neale adapted and incorporated some of the original music and retold the legend of the good king in his own inimitable style. In fact, Neale himself called it "a legend of extreme beauty" in his 1849 book *Deeds of Faith.*

Neale's translations represented almost 12 percent of the hymns in what may be the greatest and most culturally diverse hymnbook of its time, *Hymns Ancient and Modern,* which appeared in 1859.

In addition to his scholarship, he remained a humble priest and friend of the outcast and disadvantaged. Because he helped establish the first order of nuns in the Church of England since the Reformation, opponents of that action stoned him and the sisters on numerous occasions. Neale had the extraordinary ability to forgive and ignore the opposition, continuing the work that he believed he was called to do. He also served as warden of Sackville College, which was a kind of public charity for destitute elderly men. Neale was also happily married and the father of five children, one of whom became mother superior of his Sisters of St. Margaret.

His scholarly research took him to Greece and other Eastern countries. He translated hundreds of hymns from Greek and Latin, and even from some of the Scandinavian languages. Many of them were Christmas related.

For one who loved the Eastern churches, his death could not have been more timely, coming as it did on the Feast of the Transfiguration, August 6, 1866. While the Transfiguration, which celebrates the transfiguring of Jesus in the presence of His apostles Peter, James, and

John, is observed in the Roman Catholic and Anglican Churches of the West, it is not a major holy day. But in the more mystical East, it is one of the great festivals of the church calendar.

Neale was loved by the humble and lowly, who flocked to his funeral, standing in the streets and filling the chapel where his Requiem was sung. No bishops or church leaders were present, but a century later, on the centenary of his passing, the Archbishop of Canterbury, Michael Ramsey, came to honor the scholarly parson who restored to Western Christians some of the noblest hymns of the ages. (Among them are "All Glory Laud and Honor," "The Day of Resurrection," "Christ Is Made the Sure Foundation," and "Jerusalem the Golden.")

Not everyone liked "Good King Wenceslas." Percy Dearmer, author of *The Parson's Handbook* and other volumes on worship, said it had "a rather confused narrative." Other critics called it "doggerel" and "commonplace." But its popularity has grown, especially in England, and the British Post Office issued a 1973 Christmas stamp honoring "Good King Wenceslas."

As his first biographer, Eleanor Towle, once wrote, "With the exception of his writings on the Eastern church, there was probably no part of his literary work that, in retrospect, gave Neale such unmixed pleasure. His hymns not only appealed to the scholar and the student, but they quickened and inspired public and private devotion. Little children learn them by heart; the old and solitary turn to them for comfort. Christmas after Christmas his 'Good King Wenceslas' and other carols have been sung by countless young and happy voices in almost every land where the English tongue is spoken."

"GOOD KING WENCESLAS"

Good King Wenceslas looked out on the Feast of Stephen.
When the snow lay round about, deep and crisp and even;
Brightly shone the moon that night, though the frost was cruel,
When a poor man came in sight, gathering winter fuel.

"Hither, page, and stand by me if thou know'st it, telling
Yonder peasant, who is he? Where and what his dwelling?"
"Sire, he lives a good league hence, underneath the mountain,
Right against the forest fence, by Saint Agnes' fountain."

"Bring me flesh and bring me wine! Bring me pine logs hither!
Thou and I will see him dine when we bear them thither."
Page and monarch forth they went, forth they went together
Through the rude winds wild lament, and the bitter weather.

"Sire, the night is darker now, and the wind blows stronger;
Fails my heart I know not how, I can go no longer."
"Mark my footsteps, my good page, tread thou in them boldly:
Thou shalt find the winter's rage freeze thy blood less coldly."

In his master's steps he trod where the snow lay dinted;
Heat was in the very sod which the saint had printed.
Therefore, Christian men, be sure, wealth or rank possessing,
Ye who now will bless the poor, shall yourselves find blessing.

"Hark! the Herald Angels Sing"

Writing nearly a century ago in 1902, Francis Arthur Jones solemnly proclaimed, "If a general consensus of opinion were taken as to which is the most popular of all Christmas hymns, the result would probably be in favor of 'Hark the Herald Angels Sing.' From its publication in 1739, this Charles Wesley masterpiece became instantly popular, both for its profound theology and for triumphant musicality. Indeed, this was the only Christmas hymn in the dozen or so hymns appended to the *Book of Common Prayer* in 1816. Until that time, the Church of England's music consisted almost entirely of psalms, Anglican chants, the office music for settings of Holy Communion, Morning Prayer, and Evensong, but no hymns, which were seen as common and vulgar. But people in the pews wanted hymns, and eventually Anglican and Episcopal worship were enriched by the new hymnody of the eighteenth and nineteenth centuries, borrowing heavily from Methodist hymns and from early Latin and Greek hymns.

This triumphant hymn fills countless sanctuaries and chancels every Christmas. It is often sung during processions or recessions, so uplifting and vibrant are both its words and its music. Ranked eighth on a poll of Americans' favorite Christmas songs in 1998, it has always been a crowd pleaser. It has generally been the final hymn, the recessional, sung by the choir at the Festival of Nine Lessons and Carols at Kings College in Cambridge, England, perhaps the world's best-known Christmas Eve musical performance. It was, many viewers will remember, the last hymn sung by the children in *A Charlie Brown Christmas,* the award-winning program first broadcast on CBS Television in 1965.

Its author was Charles Wesley, one of the founders, with his brother John, of the Methodist Church. Wesley was extraordinarily prolific as a composer of sacred song, authoring an estimated 6,500 hymns in a fifty-year period from 1738 until his death in 1788. The Wesley brothers, whose father was a pastor in the Church of England, intended to follow in their father's footsteps, and indeed were ordained in the Church of England. Charles, while a student at Oxford University, founded a "Holy Club" to give direction and method to his spiritual life. Hence the term "Methodist" was applied to it by less than favorable observers.

Charles soon discovered his talent for writing hymns or, more properly, sacred poems that soon became hymns. Like St. Ephraem many centuries earlier, Charles excelled in expressing his religious convictions in verse and song.

In 1739 Charles, who had recently returned to England from an unhappy and disappointing time in the colony of Georgia, wrote ten stanzas of a hymn expressing his complete awe at the birth of Christ. It was immediately published in a volume called simply, *Hymns and Sacred Poems.* Like so many masterpieces, it took a while to reach acceptance and popularity.

Charles's coworker in the evangelical revival movement, George Whitefield, modified some of the words and phrases and republished it in 1753. But a full century passed before an inspired composition fit the words so perfectly that the hymn surged in popularity. The talented German composer Felix Mendelssohn had composed some triumphal music in 1840 for a commemoration of the invention of Gutenberg's movable type. Mendelssohn, whose Jewish family had converted to Christianity, was interested in religious music and had scored a musical triumph with his oratorio *Elijah*.

A few years after Mendelssohn's death at age thirty-seven, an English musical arranger, William H. Cummings, adapted the second chorus of Mendelssohn's composition and rearranged Wesley's stanzas to fit the music. It was an instantaneous success when republished in 1856.

A stamp of approval, of sorts, came when the Church of England appended "Hark! the Herald Angels Sing" to its official *Book of Common Prayer,* marking it as the only Christmas hymn officially appended for many decades. Since the Wesleys grew up in the Anglican Church and never intended to establish a new denomination, it was a rather fitting tribute. Until then the Church of England allowed only Anglican chant, metrical psalms and the polyphonic Elizabethan and Tudor music of composers like William Byrd and Thomas Tallis at divine worship. Hymns were frowned on as not dignified, too personal, and too subjective. Eventually, public opinion triumphed, and Anglican hymnody itself became world renowned.

Wesley's "Hark" was said to have been translated into more languages and to have been included in more hymnals than any other Christmas hymn by the year 1902. It certainly ranks with such other Charles Wesley hymns as "Christ the Lord Is Risen Today" and "O for a Thousand Tongues to Sing."

Its continuous popularity may well relate to the sense of certitude and acceptance it conveys. There is no theological ambiguity in its words. Christ is "the new-born King" who will reconcile God and sinners. He is "the heaven-born Prince of Peace," "by highest heaven adored." He is "the everlasting Lord, offspring of the Virgin's womb." He is indeed "the incarnate Deity," a central person of the godhead "veiled in flesh." To Charles Wesley, the baby born in a rude Bethlehem stable is the Promised One "born that man no more may die" and "born to give them second birth."

There is no other Christmas hymn that expresses so clearly the absolute conviction that the Incarnation is true as this rousing hymn written by a young man at the very beginning of his career. Not for theological searchers or doubters, "Hark! the Herald Angels Sing" represents a high Christology.

"HARK! THE HERALD ANGELS SING"

Hark! the herald angels sing,
"Glory to the newborn King!
Peace on earth, and mercy mild,
God and sinners reconciled."
Joyful, all ye nations, rise,
Join the triumph of the skies;
With the angelic host proclaim,

"Christ is born in Bethlehem."
Hark! the herald angels sing,
"Glory to the new-born King!"

Christ, by highest heaven adored,
Christ, the everlasting Lord,
Late in time behold Him come
Offspring of the Virgin's womb;
Veiled in flesh the Godhead see;
Hail the incarnate Deity!
Pleased as man with men to dwell,
Jesus, our Emmanuel:
Hark! the herald angels sing,
"Glory to the new-born King!"

Hail the heaven-born Prince of Peace!
Hail the Sun of Righteousness!
Light and life to all He brings,
Risen with healing in His wings;
Mild He lays His glory by,
Born that man no more may die,
Born to raise the sons of earth,
Born to give them second birth:
Hark! the herald angels sing,
"Glory to the new-born King."

"The Holly and the Ivy"

This popular English carol has a murky history. It sounds ancient, that is, medieval, but it may date only to

1710 in Birmingham, England. Cecil Sharp, a folklorist, added this to his 1911 book *English Folk Carols*.

This odd little ditty endows the holly and the ivy with Christian characteristics, celebrating the holly and drawing attention to its association with the foretold death of Jesus. The fourth verse refers to Christmas. The language in all six verses of this traditional song is forthright and direct.

A British film of 1954, starring Ralph Richardson, Celia Johnson, and Margaret Leighton, used this song as its title, and a boys' choir singing it made up a prominent part of the soundtrack. It was a heartwarming Christmas film about the troubled lives of a small-town vicar and his family who gather at Christmas to discover that all are beset with the kind of disappointments and sorrows that only courage and determination can solve and heal.

"THE HOLLY AND THE IVY"

The holly and the ivy,
When they are both full grown,
Of all the trees that are in the wood,
The holly bears the crown.

Refrain:

The rising of the sun
And the running of the deer,
The playing of the merry organ,
Sweet singing in the choir.

The holly bears a blossom
As white as the lily flower,
And Mary bore sweet Jesus Christ
To be our sweet Savior.

The holly bears a berry
As red as any blood,
And Mary bore sweet Jesus Christ
To do poor sinners good.

The holly bears a prickle
As sharp as any thorn,
And Mary bore sweet Jesus Christ
On Christmas Day in the morn.

The holly bears a bark
As bitter as any gall,
And Mary bore sweet Jesus Christ
For to redeem us all.

The holly and the ivy,
When they are both full grown,
Of all the trees that are in the wood,
The holly bears the crown.

"In the Bleak Mid-Winter"

Christina Rossetti was a devoutly religious person whose poetry was enhanced by her Anglo-Catholic religious convictions and sensitivities. She loved the Church of England and its High-Church orientation and character and, in fact, refused to marry a person with whom she was clearly in love because of religious differences—a very Victorian thing to do.

Her greatest poetry is her religious verse. This creates a paradox for the world of today. Writes a recent biographer, Georgina Battiscombe, "Christina's poetry is surprisingly free of any sectarian elements. Yet her Anglo-Catholicism was a basic influence on her poetry, an essential element in her individual genius."

Many critics judged her the finest woman poet of the nineteenth century. Of all her works, "In the Bleak Mid-Winter" remains the most popular, possibly because of Gustav Holst's musical setting that transformed it from a mystical poetic expression of the religion of the heart into a tender and moving Christmas carol. Georgina Battiscombe says, "Apart from this carol and the half-dozen pieces to be found in almost every anthology, Christina Rossetti's poetry is not calculated to make a strong appeal to the general public; it is at once too subtle and too sad."

Rossetti's poetry is clearly melancholy. It may reflect a lifetime of loneliness, of rejection in love, of the deaths of sisters and brothers, especially her talented and tortured brother Dante Gabriel Rossetti. She was also frequently in ill health during her life, which began in 1830 and ended in 1894.

Rossetti's upbringing was intensely intellectual, being the daughter of an Italian political refugee, Gabriele Rossetti. All four Rossetti children were writers, critics, or painters. Her brilliant but erratic brother, Dante Gabriel, was noted for the poem "The Blessed Damozel," as well as

his involvement in the Pre-Raphaelites, an artistic movement seeking a return to purity in art.

Her many religious poems include several with Christmas themes, but "In the Bleak Mid-Winter" is her Christmas masterpiece. Like many poets, she depicts a wintertime birth for Jesus, and the opening verse conveys a frigid feeling that makes the reader shiver. But the second verse has a triumphant note, heralding the Incarnation in the extraordinary line, "Our God, heaven cannot hold Him." Theologians have rarely described this seminal mystery of the Christian faith more effectively than these four lines of poetry.

The third and fourth verses are cradlesongs with an interplay between angels and the Virgin and child. The fifth and final verse seeks a positive response in terms of faith on the part of those who read or hear, returning once again to the "heart" of religion so much a part of Rossetti's poetic vision.

Christina was such a beauty that she sat as a model for the artist Holman Hunt, whose painting *The Light of the World* became a favorite of Victorian Christians. She was also the model for the Virgin Mary in her brother Dante Gabriel's famous painting, *Ecce Ancilla Domini*.

Several of Rossetti's books embody her spiritual outlook. *Called to Be Saints,* published in 1881, consists of poems dedicated to the minor festivals of the church year, mainly the days that commemorate the saints of the church. *Time Flies* is a delightful collection of readings for every day of the year and gives a full picture of her many moods.

Twelve years after her death, British composer Gustav Holst wrote the music to "In the Bleak Mid-Winter," guaranteeing its life as a hymn with considerable appeal. Holst was born in Cheltenham, England, in 1874 to a family of Swedish musicians. He dabbled in Hindu literature and music and wrote a strange 1920 work, *The Hymn of Jesus*, based on apocryphal gospels rather than the New Testament canon. But he did contribute several hymns to the *English Hymnal* before his death in 1934.

"IN THE BLEAK MID-WINTER"

In the bleak mid-winter, frosty wind made moan;
Earth stood hard as iron, water like a stone;
Snow had fallen, snow on snow, snow on snow,
In the bleak mid-winter, long ago.

Our God, heaven cannot hold Him, nor earth sustain;
Heaven and earth shall flee away, when He comes to reign;
In the bleak mid-winter, a stable-place sufficed
The Lord God Almighty, Jesus Christ.

Enough for Him whom cherubim worship night and day,
A breastful of milk and a mangerful of hay;
Enough for Him whom angels fall down before,
The ox and ass and camel which adore.

Angels and archangels may have gathered there,
Cherubim and seraphim thronged the air;
But His mother only, in her maiden bliss
Worshiped the Beloved with a kiss.

What can I give Him, poor as I am?
If I were a shepherd, I would bring a lamb;
If I were a wise man, I would do my part;
Yet what I can I give Him—Give my heart.

"Joy to the World"

"Joy to the World" is one of the most popular of Christmas carols, ranking fifth on the list of favorites in a 1998 national survey conducted by Ohio University. It also has the unusual distinction of not being intended as a Christmas hymn, either in the words or in the music.

Isaac Watts, who wrote perhaps six or seven hundred poems that have been set to music and reconstituted as hymns, was its author. Based on Psalm 98, rather than on the Nativity narrative, it appeared in Watts's 1719 book *Psalms of David, Imitated in the Language of the New Testament.* It was not always seen as a Christmas hymn, and in Episcopal hymnals from 1874 to 1940 it was listed as a general hymn. In practice, it is sung only at Christmastime.

A native of Southampton, England, Watts was born there in 1674. A pious young man, he prepared early for the ministry. Watts's father was a deacon in the Independent Church, an evangelical group. He also owned a boardinghouse and was imprisoned twice for religious dissent. The family's mother carried Isaac in her arms when she sang hymns outside the prison to encourage her husband.

Young Isaac complained about the boring and listless hymns in his congregation, and his father challenged him to write some better ones. This he did, and at age fifteen his hymns were being sung by his church. On his twenty-first birthday he preached a sermon at the Independent Church in Mark Lane, London, where he was pastor for a while.

The lifelong bachelor had a natural talent for writing verse, supposedly from the age of seven until his death at age seventy-four in 1748. Says Ernest Emurian, "He gave Christendom some of the noblest and most sublime hymns in the English language." This includes the profoundly moving Lenten/Good Friday hymn, "When I Survey the Wondrous Cross."

As seems so common among artistic temperaments, Watts experienced ill health. He resigned from his pulpit in 1712 and accepted an invitation to recuperate for a week at the estate of Sir Thomas Abney, the Lord Mayor of London. He stayed thirty-six years and became the private chaplain of the household. Watts's hymns were immensely popular with some conservative Christians but unpopular with others. His legacy has endured.

The music that commonly accompanies "Joy to the World" is by Lowell Mason, an American Presbyterian. Mason was born in Dedham, Massachusetts, in 1792, and his youth was given largely to music. By age sixteen he was leading the village choir and conducting singing schools for children. In 1812 he moved to Savannah, Georgia, where he worked in a bank and became organist and choirmaster for the First Presbyterian Church. Moving to Boston in 1827, Mason was elected president of the Handel and Haydn Society, one of America's oldest classical music groups, and served as choir director at Lyman Beecher's Bowdoin Street Church. A lifetime of teaching music, arranging hymns, and publishing song books led to his receiving an honorary degree from New York University. He died in Orange, New Jersey, in 1872.

Herbert Wernecke paid tribute to "Joy to the World" in these words: "It is a great hymn of Advent and of the Nativity. We feel all nature thrilling with joy at the Savior's birth. It is a forceful expression of missionary zeal and prophetic triumph."

"JOY TO THE WORLD!"

Joy to the world! The Lord is come:
Let earth receive her King;
Let every heart prepare Him room,
And heaven and nature sing,
And heaven and nature sing,
And heaven, and heaven and nature sing.

Joy to the world! The Savior reigns:
Let men their songs employ,
While fields and floods, rocks, hills and plains,
Repeat the sounding joy,
Repeat the sounding joy,
Repeat, repeat the sounding joy.

No more let sins and sorrows grow,
Nor thorns infest the ground;
He comes to make His blessings flow
Far as the curse is found,
Far as the curse is found,
Far as, far as the curse is found.

He rules the world with truth and grace,
And makes the nations prove
The glories of His righteousness,

> *And wonders of His love,*
> *And wonders of His love,*
> *And wonders, and wonders of His love.*

"Love Came Down at Christmas"

Percy Dearmer, one of the compilers of the classic *Oxford Book of Carols,* called this a "gem, where so much is said in so little space." Herbert Wernecke, a pioneer popularizer of Christmas culture, praised it for its "childlike vividness of devotion and consecrated trust."

A late poem by the talented Christina Rossetti, this charming and tender verse has frequently been included in anthologies of Christmas poetry. It appeared in her 1885 collection, *Time Flies.*

It is not surprising that this poem eventually became a hymn. Several melodies are used for this hymn. The most common is an Irish folk melody from County Donegal, the windswept, rainy, and beautiful northwest region of Ireland. Herbert Wernecke wrote that "the music is of rare beauty with a quiet and somewhat medieval flavor."

Another popular adaptation is by Reginald Owen Morris, who was born in the cathedral town of York, England. His melody appeared in the 1925 book *Songs of Praise.* Morris taught at the Curtis Institute of Music in Philadelphia from 1926 to 1931. The Methodists added this song to their hymnal in the 1930s.

"LOVE CAME DOWN AT CHRISTMAS"

Love came down at Christmas,
Love all lovely, Love Divine;
Love was born at Christmas,
Star and angels gave the sign.

Worship we the Godhead,
Love Incarnate, Love Divine;
Worship we our Jesus:
But where-with for sacred sign?

Love shall be our token,
Love be yours and love be mine,
Love to God and all men,
Love for plea and gift and sign.

"On Christmas Night All Christians Sing"

Generally called "The Sussex Carol" because it was collected by folklorists in the English country of Sussex, this lively carol appeared in 1684 in a charming volume called *A Small Garland of Pious and Godly Songs.* It was then simply called "Another Short Carol for Christmas Day."

Its author may have been Luke Wadding, a Catholic bishop consecrated for work in Ireland but residing in exile in Ghent in what is now Belgium. The religious wars then raging in the British Isles made life difficult and uncertain for clergy of all ranks, particularly those on the losing side of the conflicts.

Perhaps this is why one can read between the lines in Wadding's verses. He urges his listeners to put away sadness and to feel joy, even mirth, at the incomparable news of the birth of a "new-born King" and "Redeemer." Darkness gives way to light. The author seems to be saying that whatever difficulties may now be evident in the lives of humanity, their ultimate destiny is safe. No one need have fear anymore.

"The Sussex Carol" underwent many textual changes over the centuries. By the early 1900s it had become a true folk song, relegated to singers in the rural countryside of England. Ralph Vaughan Williams and his colleague Cecil Sharp heard a certain Mrs. Verrall of Monks Gate in West Sussex sing this carol one day in 1904, and they wrote down the words and the music. While there are different musical settings, the words reflect a confident spirit and a certitude that the Christmas event had transformed the world.

"On Christmas Night All Christians Sing"

On Christmas night all Christians sing,
To hear the news the angels bring:
News of great joy, news of great mirth,
News of our merciful King's birth.

Then why should men on earth be so sad,
Since our Redeemer made us glad

When from our sin He set us free,
All for to gain our liberty?

When sin departs before His grace,
Then life and health come in its place;
Angels and men with joy may sing,
All for to see the new-born King.

All out of darkness we have light,
Which made the angels sing this night:
"Glory to God and peace to men,
Now and for evermore, Amen."

"Once in Royal David's City"

"Once in Royal David's City" began as a children's Sunday school song and has seen new life as a grand processional hymn for Christmas Eve. In England it has become the traditional opening of Christmas when a solo caroler sings the opening lines at the Festival of Nine Lessons and Carols at Kings College Chapel in Cambridge. Broadcast on radio throughout the United Kingdom, it has given sustenance and hope and renewed the faith of generations, even in the darkest days of history, since it was inaugurated shortly after the First World War.

The hymn's author, Mrs. Cecil Frances Alexander (formerly Fanny Humphreys), was a Dublin-born Sunday school teacher who tried to communicate the teachings of the Christian faith with simple verse and song. She wrote this song to explain the third article of the Apostles' Creed, "conceived by the Holy Ghost, born of the Virgin Mary." It has been suggested that she wrote her children's hymns because a godchild complained that he could not understand the catechism. Her husband was an Anglican rector who became a bishop, and after her death the Archbishop of the Church of Ireland.

This hymn of six stanzas has distinct narrative divisions. The first two verses retell the Nativity story in simple, clear, and concise prose. Verses three and four describe His "wondrous childhood," where "He would honor and obey the lowly maiden in whose gentle arms He lay." Mrs. Alexander then reminds children that they should emulate Jesus by being "mild and obedient." She also reminds them that the little Jesus was "weak and helpless" and knew "tears and smiles like us." The final stanzas look to the glorified Jesus in heaven where "our eyes at last shall see Him, through His own redeeming love."

Canon Frank Colquhoun, author of several profound reflections on hymns as vehicles of wisdom and awe, noted that the ending of this hymn "followed the conventional pattern of her time because Victorian hymn-writers were very 'heavenly-minded' and customarily finished their hymns with a verse or two about the beatific vision and the life everlasting."

Colquhoun praised Alexander's style because "she uses simple language which a child can understand and writes the sort of poetry which a child can easily learn and remember." He adds, "Most important of all, she seeks to capture interest by appealing to the imagination. She does not begin a hymn with abstract theology. She begins by painting a picture, by telling a story, and against that background she develops her teaching."

The carol first appeared in her *Hymns for Little Children* in 1848. When added to the *English Hymnal*, it was placed in the catechism section, not among the Christmas hymns, and with the notation, "suitable also for adults." The *Episcopal Hymnal* for the U.S. added it in 1874 but placed it among the general hymns.

Among her other well-loved hymns are "All Things Bright and Beautiful," a cheerful hymn used on many occasions, and the somber Good Friday hymn, "There Is a Green Hill Far Away." Still popular are her "Jesus Calls Us," a conversion and missionary hymn for St. Andrew's Day, and a retelling of St. Patrick's "I Bind Unto Myself Today" for Trinity Sunday.

Mrs. Alexander's hymns and poems made her immensely popular during her lifetime. Upon her death on October 12, 1895, cathedral bells tolled. Ninety-two clergymen attended her funeral. Shops were closed, and the streets of Northern Ireland's second largest city, Derry, were thronged with mourners.

Her most recent biographer, Valerie Wallace, wrote, "Fanny's unassuming piety and kindness were like lamps unremarked until they were extinguished." Her great hymns, including "Once in Royal David's City," are "the enduring monuments to her life," Wallace adds.

She devoted all of her royalties to the poor and disadvantaged children of her beloved Ireland. Today a stained-glass window in St. Columb's Cathedral in Londonderry (Derry), Northern Ireland, honors "Once in

Royal David's City" (and two of her other hymns). She is buried a short distance away from the green hills that inspired her.

"ONCE IN ROYAL DAVID'S CITY"

Once in royal David's city
Stood a lowly cattle shed,
Where a mother laid her Baby
In a manger for His bed:
Mary was that mother mild,
Jesus Christ her little child.

He came down to earth from heaven,
Who is God and Lord of all,
And His shelter was a stable,
And His cradle was a stall;
With the poor, and mean, and lowly,
Lived on earth our Savior holy.

And through all His wondrous childhood
He would honor and obey,
Love and watch the lowly maiden,
In whose gentle arms He lay:
Christian children all must be
Mild, obedient, good as He.

For He is our childhood's pattern:
Day by day like us He grew,
He was little, weak, and helpless,
Tears and smiles like us He knew;

And He feeleth for our sadness,
And He shareth in our gladness.

And our eyes at last shall see Him,
Through His own redeeming love,
For that child so dear and gentle
Is our Lord in heaven above;
And He leads His children on
To the place where He is gone.

"See, Amid the Winter's Snow"

This lovely Victorian poem was written by Edward Caswall, an Anglican priest who became a Roman Catholic. It remains more popular in England than in America, but it deserves a wider audience, since it has the qualities of simplicity and directness that make it suitable for children as well as adults. Easy to sing, it appeared first in Caswall's *Easy Hymn Tunes* in 1851.

While retaining a simplicity of style, it contains some elegant language, referring to Jesus as "the tender Lamb" "promised from eternal years" and observing that only "a tender love" would cause the Eternal One to come "down to such a world as this."

Caswall translated many of the great Latin hymns, including St. Bernard of Clairvaux's "Jesus, the Very Thought of Thee." He spent the last eighteen years of his life working under Cardinal John Henry Newman at the Oratory of St. Philip Neri.

The music is by Sir John Goss, a composer and organist at St. Paul's Cathedral in London from 1838 until 1872. He was knighted by Queen Victoria and died in 1880.

"SEE, AMID THE WINTER'S SNOW"

See, amid the winter's snow,
Born for us on earth below,
See, the tender Lamb appears,
Promised from eternal years!

Refrain:

Hail thou ever blessed morn!
Hail, Redemption's happy dawn!
Sing through all Jerusalem:
Christ is born in Bethlehem!

Lo! within a manger lies
He who built the starry skies,
He who, throned in height sublime,
Sits amid the Cherubim.

Say, ye holy shepherds, say:
What your joyful news today?
Wherefore have ye left your sheep
On the lonely mountain steep?

As we watched at dead of night,
Lo! we saw a wondrous light;
Angels, singing "Peace on earth,"
Told us of the Savior's birth.

Sacred Infant, all divine,
What a tender love was Thine
Thus to come from highest bliss
Down to such a world as this!

Teach, oh teach us, holy Child,
By Thy face so meek and mild,
Teach us to resemble Thee
In Thy sweet humility!

"The Snow Lay on the Ground"

This charming carol, mixing English and Latin, is relatively modern. Its true and complete history is unknown, but it is called an "Anglo-Irish carol," suggesting authorship among those Irish gentry who maintained close connections with the English establishment.

It appeared in an 1862 book called *The Crown of Jesus* under the label "Christmas Carol, sung in Rome by the Pifferari from the Abruzzi mountains." Could this have been an Italian bagpipe song brought back to Ireland by a traveler with musical inclinations?

The Latin refrain, *Venite adoramus Dominum,* is very singable. It was harmonized in 1941 by Leo Sowerby, an American composer, organist, and choirmaster. Sowerby won the Pulitzer Prize for music in 1946 for his oratorio, *Canticle of the Sun,* based on the life of St. Francis of Assisi.

"THE SNOW LAY ON THE GROUND"

The snow lay on the ground,
The stars shone bright,
When Christ our Lord was born
On Christmas night.

Refrain:
Venite adoremus
Dominum;
Venite adoremus
Dominum.
'Twas Mary, daughter pure
Of holy Anne,
That brought into this world
The God made man.
She laid Him in a stall
At Bethlehem;
The ass and oxen shared
The roof with them.

Saint Joseph, too, was by
To tend the child;
To guard Him, and protect
His mother mild:
The angels hovered round,
And sang this song,
Venite adoremus
Dominum.

And thus that manger poor
Became a throne;
For He whom Mary bore
Was God the Son.
O come, then, let us join
The heavenly host,
To praise the Father, Son,
And Holy Ghost.

"Thou Didst Leave Thy Throne"

"Thou Didst Leave Thy Throne" is an unusual carol in several respects. For one thing, its primary biblical reference is to Luke 2:7: "There was no room for them in the inn," always a favorite among poets, preachers, and short-story writers. Only the first two verses deal with the Nativity. Verses three and four refer to the ministry and death of Jesus, while the fifth refers to His final coming in glory.

Still, it has received some popularity over the years and is an admirable example of subjective "heart religion," designed to stir emotions and produce a favorable response on the part of the listener. This lovely hymn was at first privately printed for use of the parishioners at St. Mark's Church in Brighton, England, in 1864. Its use spread to all denominations.

Its author, Emily Elizabeth Steele Elliott, was the daughter of an English rector and the niece of Charlotte Elliott, whose musical fame is assured by her popular invitation hymn, "Just As I Am, Without One Plea." Emily Elliott, who lived in England in the nineteenth century, wrote more than two hundred hymns. Her other connection with Christmas is her early translation of "Silent Night" into English. (She may have been the first translator.)

The music for this hymn was composed by Timothy Matthews, an organist and clergyman of the Church of England.

"THOU DIDST LEAVE THY THRONE"

Thou didst leave Thy throne and Thy kingly crown
When Thou camest to earth for me;
But in Bethlehem's home was there found no room
For Thy holy nativity.
O come to my heart, Lord Jesus!
There is room in my heart for Thee.

Heaven's arches rang when the angels sang,
Proclaiming Thy royal degree;
But in lowly birth didst Thou come to earth,
And in great humility.
O come to my heart, Lord Jesus!
There is room in my heart for Thee.

The foxes found rest, and the birds had their nest
In the shade of the forest tree;
But Thy couch was the sod, O Thou Son of God,
In the desert of Galilee.

O come to my heart, Lord Jesus!
There is room in my heart for Thee.

Thou camest, O Lord, with the living Word
That should set Thy people free;
But with mocking scorn, and with crown of thorn,
They bore Thee to Calvary.
O come to my heart, Lord Jesus!
Thy cross is my only plea.

When the heavens shall ring, and the angels sing
At Thy coming to victory,
Let Thy voice call me home, saying, "Yet there is room,
There is room at My side for thee."
And my heart shall rejoice, Lord Jesus,
When Thou comest and callest for me.

"What Child Is This"

William Chatterton Dix was an insurance agent whose avocation was poetry and hymn writing. He wrote the tender, meditative words to this song when he was a young man. It has a haunting quality and provokes both reflection and introspection on the part of those who hear it sung, often with guitar accompaniment.

This wonderful ballad includes some interesting spiritual language, such as, "The silent Word is pleading," a reference to the babe in swaddling clothes who is the Logos, the Word of Salvation promised and now born in human flesh. Dix also urges all "loving hearts" to "enthrone" the "King of kings" who brings salvation to those who believe in Him.

Dix published his last book of poems, *Seekers of a City,* in 1878, twenty years before his death. His health, which had always been precarious, improved during the last three decades of his life. One of his hymns, "Come unto Me, Ye Weary and I Will Give You Rest," was written during a miraculous recovery from a life-threatening illness in 1867.

Sir John Stainer, a Victorian-era composer of church music, harmonized "What Child Is This?" and transformed it into a hymn tune. It is set to the music of an old English folk song called "Greensleeves," which was popular in Shakespeare's time. Shakespeare mentions it twice in his *Merry Wives of Windsor.* In the seventeenth century it was used as the melody for a New Year's carol, "The Old Year Now Away Is Fled."

Stainer, whose music was almost synonymous with English cathedrals, is perhaps best known for "God So Loved the World." Stainer was a choirmaster who made London's St. Paul's Cathedral Choir one of the greatest in the world. He was a musicologist and professor of music at Oxford. Fittingly, he died in 1901, the same year as Queen Victoria, who had knighted him thirteen years before, when failing eyesight caused his resignation from St. Paul's.

"WHAT CHILD IS THIS?"

What Child is this, who, laid to rest,
On Mary's lap is sleeping?
Whom angels greet with anthems sweet,
While shepherds watch are keeping?

Refrain:
This, this is Christ the King,
Whom shepherds guard and angels sing:
Haste, haste to bring Him laud,
The Babe, the Son of Mary!

Why lies He in such mean estate
Where ox and ass are feeding?
Good Christian, fear: for sinners here
The silent Word is pleading.

So bring Him incense, gold, and myrrh,
Come, peasant, king to own Him;
The King of kings salvation brings,
Let loving hearts enthrone Him.

"While Shepherds Watched Their Flocks by Night"

"While Shepherds Watched Their Flocks by Night" is one of the earliest English carols for Christmas. It was written by Nahum Tate, an Irishman born in Dublin in 1652 and a graduate of the city's renowned Trinity College.

Tate wrote for the stage and collaborated with John Dryden, but he was never able to achieve fame and fortune as a dramatist. Still, he had friends in high places and succeeded in becoming poet laureate in 1692 and royal historiographer in 1702.

A religious man, he produced a *New Version of the Psalms of David*, in collaboration with Nicholas Brady in 1696. These were metrical versions of the Psalms intended for divine worship. "While Shepherds Watched Their Flocks by Night" is a literal paraphrase of Luke 2:8–15, and its popularity was immediate. It was one of only six hymns, and the only Christmas hymn, then permitted in the worship of the Church of England. Canticles and psalms were the only musical forms then observed. It is also the only one of the six that has survived three centuries later. Tate called this poem the "Song of the Angels, at the Nativity of Our Blessed Savior." When the American Episcopal Church issued its first prayer book in 1789, this was one of twenty-seven hymns specifically authorized for public worship. The popularity of this sincere and straightforward retelling of the shepherds' role in the Nativity story has been widespread throughout the Christian world.

Thomas Est composed the solemn and stately tune generally used in England. Some hymnals use an arrangement by Handel. Richard Storrs Willis composed the music generally sung to Tate's words in the United States. Willis was a talented musician, a music critic, and an author. He was a vestryman at the Church of the Transfiguration in New York City, an Episcopal church noted for its majestic music and liturgy and openness to members of the artistic and theatrical community.

The fate of Nahum Tate shows that artistic accomplishment does not always bring fame or contentment. Alexander Pope referred to him as "poor Tate—always a sorrowful appearance and in a terrible muddle," and Robert Southey called him "the lowest of the Laureates." He was always poor and died penniless, while hiding from his creditors, in London in 1715. Tate may have died in poverty, but he enriched the world for all time with his wonderful hymn.

"WHILE SHEPHERDS WATCHED THEIR FLOCKS BY NIGHT"

While shepherds watched their flocks by night,
All seated on the ground,
The angel of the Lord came down,
And glory shone around,
And glory shone around.

"Fear not!" said he; for mighty dread
Had seized their troubled mind.
"Glad tidings of great joy I bring,
To you and all mankind,
To you and all mankind.

"To you, in David's town, this day
Is born of David's line,
The Savior who is Christ the Lord;
And this shall be the sign,
And this shall be the sign.

"The heavenly Babe you there shall find

To human view displayed,
All meanly wrapped in swathing bands,
And in a manger laid,
And in a manger laid."

Thus spake the seraph; and forthwith
Appeared a shining throng
Of angels praising God on high,
Who thus addressed their song;
Who thus addressed their song:

"All glory be to God on high,
And to the earth be peace:
Good will henceforth from heaven to men,
Begin and never cease!
Begin and never cease!"

III

FRENCH AND SPANISH
SONGS AND HYMNS

French carols have a charm and frivolity that reminds one of the santons, the carefully fashioned figures for the crèche found in Provence. French Christmas music reflects the character of a nation and people who love Christmas and observe it with gusto.

This section features five French and Spanish songs, including the more solemn and majestic "The First Noel" and "O Holy Night."

"The Angel Gabriel"

This lovely, lilting carol comes from the Basque County of northern Spain and southernmost France. It is one of the few carols to focus on the Annunciation, which has always delighted poets and painters. Its soft, meditative quality makes it appealing.

The English translation comes from Sabine Baring-Gould, one of those extraordinary nineteenth-century English clerics who dabbled in antiquarian research, puttered around in old rectories and libraries, and wrote dozens of books. His best-known contribution to hymnology is "Onward, Christian Soldiers," which for many decades has been an immensely popular hymn in England and America. An Anglican priest, he wrote fiction, biography, history, poetry, and the fifteen-volume *Lives of the Saints*. He was blessed with longevity, living from 1834 to 1924.

"THE ANGEL GABRIEL"

The angel Gabriel from heaven came,
His wings as drifted snow, his eyes as flame:
"All hail," said he, "thou lowly maiden Mary,
Most highly favored lady!" Gloria!

"For known a blessed Mother thou shalt be;
All generations laud and honor thee:
Thy son shall be Emmanuel, by seers foretold.
Most highly favored lady!" Gloria!

Then gentle Mary meekly bowed her head;
"To me be as it pleaseth God!" she said.
"My soul shall laud and magnify His holy Name."
Most highly favored lady! Gloria!

Of her Emmanuel, the Christ, was born,
In Bethlehem, all on a Christmas morn;
And Christian folk throughout the world will ever say:
"Most highly favored lady! Gloria!"

"Angels We Have Heard on High"

This is most likely an eighteenth-century French carol of unknown origin, although scholars have traced its earliest popularity to France and Quebec. It is an example of a noël, a lighthearted French carol. By the 1840s its popularity was well established. It became popular in England as a result of Bishop James Chadwick, who translated it for his *Holy Family Hymns* in 1860.

Two Americans, Edward Shippen Barnes and Earl Marlott, adapted and arranged the music and text for a 1937 hymnal. It sometimes replaces the "Gloria" at Christmas Eve services.

ANGELS WE HAVE HEARD ON HIGH

Angels we have heard on high,
Singing sweetly o'er the plains,
And the mountains in reply
Echoing their joyous strains:

Refrain:
Gloria in excelsis Deo!

Shepherds, why this jubilee?
Why these joyous strains prolong?
What the gladsome tidings be
Which inspire your heavenly song?

Come to Bethlehem and see
Him whose birth the angels sing;

Come, adore on bended knee
Christ the Lord, the new-born King!

See Him in a manger laid,
Whom the choirs of angels praise;
Mary, Joseph, lend your aid,
While our hearts in love we raise.

"Ding! Dong! Merrily on High"

This jaunty tune was originally a sixteenth-century French folk melody. It appears in a 1588 book about

ballet dancing, of all things. It had no association with Christmas until George Ratcliffe Woodward, an Anglican vicar who served numerous parishes throughout England, wrote some simple, joyous words that convey the flavor of the ringing of bells at Christmas.

Woodward, who lived from 1848 to 1934, loved Christmas carols, and he specialized in writing new words to centuries-old folk tunes. He published a number of carol books, including one for Easter and Ascensiontide, though most of them are Christmas collections.

In "Ding! Dong! Merrily on High," Woodward deliberately used words that might have suggested an early historical period, though it is likely that he wrote these happy phrases in the early twentieth century. He mixed Latin and English phrases, and his words seem to be aimed at carol singers and bell ringers, whose contributions to Christmas festivity have been much appreciated. Linking the bells of heaven to the steeple bells on earth gives this little carol a sense of the eternal.

"DING! DONG! MERRILY ON HIGH"

Ding! dong! merrily on high,
In heaven the bells are ringing
Ding dong, verily the sky
Is riv'n with angel-singing:
Gloria ... Hosanna in excelsis.

E'en so here below, below
Let steeple bells be swungen

And io, io, io
By priest and people sungen:
Gloria … Hosanna in excelsis.

Pray you, dutifully prime
Your matin chime, ye ringers;
May you beautifully rhyme
Your evetime song, ye singers:
Gloria … Hosanna in excelsis.

"The First Noel"

This delightfully singable carol, with its refrain "Born is the King of Israel," has an anonymous lyricist and an anonymous musician. It probably entered the repertory in the sixteenth or seventeenth century, although carols appeared as early as the fourteenth century. The original carols were dance tunes as well as songs and were written to grace secular occasions (such as the May carols for the Maypole dances) as well as church festivals. It is probably of French origin.

Of "The First Noel" Ernest Emurian wrote, "The anonymous poet and the unknown musician who composed the music did a thorough job of their composition, because their Christmas carol has been a popular one for almost three centuries, and is about the oldest familiar carol in the English language." It was first published in William Sandys' *Christmas Carols, Ancient and Modern* in 1833, one of the first anthologies devoted to Christmas music.

The inspiration for the author was Luke 2:10: "Fear not: for, behold, I bring you good tidings of great joy, which shall be to all people." The shepherds and wise men are the primary actors in this drama, and the poet has taken some poetic license with the New Testament text by having the shepherds see the star. The last verse links the birth of Jesus with His death, referring to "our heavenly Lord, that hath made heaven and earth of naught, and with His blood mankind hath bought."

Always popular with the people and among strolling carolers, "The First Noel" did not enter the *Episcopal Hymnal* until 1916, a bit later than some other carols. Early versions spelled it "Nowell," the Old English form of the French noel.

"THE FIRST NOEL"

The first Noel, the angels did say
Was to certain poor shepherds in fields as they lay;
In fields as they lay, keeping their sheep
On a cold winter's night that was so deep.

Refrain:

Noel, Noel, Noel, Noel
Born is the King of Israel.

They looked up and saw a star
Shining in the east beyond them far,
And to the earth it gave great light,
And so it continued both day and night.

And by the light of that same star
Three wise men came from country far,
To seek for a king was their intent,
And to follow the star wherever it went.

This star drew nigh to the northwest,
O'er Bethlehem it took its rest,
And there it did both stop and stay
Right over the place where Jesus lay.

Then entered in those wise men three
Full reverently upon their knee,
And offered there in His presence,
Their gold, and myrrh, and frankincense.

Then let us all with one accord
Sing praises to our heavenly Lord;
That hath made heaven and earth of naught,
And with His blood mankind hath bought.

"O Holy Night"

In a survey of the most popular Christmas carols conducted in 1998 by Ohio University, this reverent song ranked second in popularity. Its origins suggest that its popularity arose from the grass roots of society and spread throughout the world.

"O Holy Night" was born in the Rhone Valley of France. An unusual circumstance of events brought it to life. In the town of Roquemaure, a wine dealer and part-time poet, Placide Clappeau, was asked by the local parish priest to compose a Christmas poem to take to Adolphe-Charles Adam, a composer in Paris. Clappeau was a friend of a local singer, a Madame Laurey, who in turn knew Adam. Clappeau agreed with this unusual request and wrote the poem that became this song while on a train to Paris on December 3, 1847.

Clappeau presented the poem to Adam, then the rage of Paris because of his popular ballet, *Giselle*. Adam also loved comic opera and produced about two operas a year until his death in 1856. Like many composers, he struggled financially in his later years and taught music at the Paris Conservatory to make ends meet. Adam liked Clappeau's poem and took only a few days to write the music. "O Holy Night" then received its first performance at Christmas Eve Midnight Mass in Roquemaure.

This, shall we say, is the accepted version of how it all happened, a series of surprising coincidences that strain credulity, to be sure. Would a famous composer like Adam have even bothered to see an obscure wine merchant with a poem in his pocket? Still, stranger things have happened, and the world of Christmas music has been enriched by this creation.

Within a few years the song was published in London. Its popularity grew in many nations. An American music critic and journalist, John Sullivan Dwight, wrote what is probably the best-known English language version.

While the first two verses celebrate the night of the Nativity, the third verse speaks of peace and liberation of humankind from oppression and slavery, which still existed in many lands when Clappeau wrote the words.

The carol received a burst of publicity during the Franco-Prussian War of 1870–71. This story is probably a legend, but it has been told and retold so many times that it has taken on the aura of truth. The story goes that a French soldier emerged from his trenches on Christmas Eve and sang "Cantique de Noel" (Song of Christmas), the French title of "O Holy Night." It so moved the opposing German army that a German soldier arose and sang "Von Himmel Hoch" (From Heaven Above to Earth I Come), Martin Luther's beloved carol. Thus a brief Christmas truce was achieved through the medium of music and because of a shared religious faith. Whether true or not, it reflects the joy of music and its power to inspire even in the darkest of days.

Surprisingly, "O Holy Night" lost favor in France during the political turmoil of the 1930s. *The Oxford Companion to Music* relates that "O Holy Night" "began to find itself excluded from the churches by one French bishop after another, on the ground of 'its lack of musical taste and total absence of the spirit of religion.'" Those who love the song today feel that it embodies the best of the religious spirit and enriches the holiday season.

"O HOLY NIGHT"

O holy night, the stars are brightly shining;
It is the night of the dear Savior's birth!
Long lay the world in sin and error pining,
Till He appeared and the soul felt its worth.
A thrill of hope, the weary world rejoices,
For yonder breaks a new and glorious morn.

Refrain:

Fall on your knees, O hear the angel voices!
O night divine, O night when Christ was born!
O night, O holy night, O night divine!

Led by the light of faith serenely beaming,
With glowing hearts by His cradle we stand.
So led by light of a star sweetly gleaming,
Here came the wise men from Orient land.
The King of kings lay thus in lowly manger,
In all our trials born to be our friend!

Truly He taught us to love one another;
His law is love and His Gospel is peace.
Chains shall He break for the slave is our brother
And in His Name all oppression shall cease.
Sweet hymns of joy in grateful chorus raise we,
Let all within us praise His holy Name!

IV

GERMAN AND AUSTRIAN SONGS AND HYMNS

German carols have a warmth and tenderness that reflect the German people's heartfelt enthusiasm for the Advent, Christmas, and Epiphany seasons. German Christmas music is both festive and solemn, illustrative of the many moods associated with the Nativity holiday.

German music is radiant and beautiful. It has reverent and prayerful qualities that enrich holiday celebrations. The same is true of Austria, the tiny land that gave us "Still, Still, Still" and, above all, "Silent Night."

Nine songs from this region of Central Europe are included in this section.

"All My Heart This Night Rejoices"

This once-popular German hymn written by Paulus Gerhardt, a cleric of the Lutheran Church who lived in an era of great turmoil, first appeared in a 1653 hymnbook. When he was twelve years old, Swedish soldiers burned his hometown during the Thirty Years' War, and the horrible memories of this devastation were reflected in some of his early poems.

Born in 1607 near Wittenberg and the son of the mayor (burgomaster), Gerhardt was ordained in 1651 and spent six years in the small town of Mittenwalde. He wrote this profoundly moving hymn at a time of great personal trial and suffering.

He later was pastor of the Church of St. Nicholas in Berlin, but he was dismissed because of his opposition to a church union scheme effected by the government. No stranger to sorrow, Gerhardt lost his wife and four of his five children. With his one surviving child, he went to the small town of Luebben to preach and write hymns until his death on June 7, 1676. One of his most popular hymns is the moving Lenten classic, "O Sacred Head, Sore Wounded."

While immensely popular in Germany, "All My Heart This Night Rejoices" did not appear in England and America until Catherine Winkworth translated it in 1855 and reduced the number of stanzas from fifteen to ten. Today only a few are generally sung. Miss Winkworth, an educator fluent in German, translated a number of beautiful German hymn classics, including "Deck Thyself, My Soul with Gladness," "Now Thank We All Our God," and "Lift Up Your Heads, Ye Mighty Gates," thus enriching hymnals in the English-speaking world.

Winkworth devoted her life both to music and to the promotion of higher education for women. One bishop said she had a "combination of rare ability and great knowledge with a certain tender and sympathetic refinement." A tablet on the wall of Bristol Cathedral in England honors her memory with the observation that she "opened a new source of light, consolation and strength in many thousand homes."

She may have translated more great German hymns into English than any other scholar, and her book *Christian Singers of Germany* brought the history of German chorale music to the English-speaking world.

Herbert Wernecke called "All My Heart This Night Rejoices" "a glorious series of Christmas thoughts laid as a garland on the manger of Bethlehem."

"ALL MY HEART THIS NIGHT REJOICES"

All my heart this night rejoices
As I hear, far and near,
Sweetest angel voices.
"Christ is born," their choirs are singing,
Till the air everywhere
Now with joy is ringing.

Hark! A voice from yonder manger,
Soft and sweet, doth entreat:
"Flee from woe and danger!
Brethren, come! From all doth grieve you,
You are freed; all you need
I will surely give you."

Come, then, let us hasten yonder!
Here let all, great and small,
Kneel in awe and wonder!
Love Him who with love is yearning!
Hail the star that from far
Bright with hope is burning!

Thee, dear Lord, with heed I'll cherish;
Live to Thee faithfully:
Dying, never perish;
But abide in life eternal
Where with Thee I shall be
Filled with joy supernal.

"Break Forth, O Beauteous Heavenly Light"

A classic example of the German Lutheran chorale, this triumphal hymn is actually only the ninth stanza of a seventeenth-century Christmas hymn by Johann Rist. With its text based on Isaiah 9:2–7, it is best known because Bach used it in his *Christmas Oratorio*.

A pastor in several German towns, Rist endured great suffering during the Thirty Years' War, which ravaged his homeland. A dedicated writer, he was named poet laureate by Emperor Ferdinand III in 1645. Rist wrote poems and stage plays, as well as numerous hymns.

"BREAK FORTH, O BEAUTEOUS HEAVENLY LIGHT"

Break forth, O beauteous heavenly light,
And usher in the morning;
Ye shepherds, shrink not with affright,
But hear the angel's warning.
This child, now weak in infancy,
Our confidence and joy shall be,
The power of Satan breaking,
Our peace eternal making.

"From Heaven High"

"From Heaven High" was written by Martin Luther, the great German Reformer, for his family's Christmas Eve celebration, probably in 1534 or 1535. Originally, different parts of the hymn were sung by a solo male voice impersonating an angel, and a children's choir. The melody used is German, and its composer is anonymous, though some scholars think Luther also wrote the music. A Scottish clergyman, John Wedderburn, published an English translation in 1539 in his *Gude and Godlie Ballades*, written in an old Scots dialect.

Canon Winfred Douglas, an American Episcopalian musicologist, linguist, and parish priest, rendered a new translation in 1939, which is used in some hymnals today. Douglas was an organist, a mountain climber, a devotee of Native American culture, an author, and a

lecturer in church music. He translated and arranged dozens of hymns for the Episcopal hymnals of 1916 and 1940. After his death at age seventy-seven in 1944, his extensive library of books about church music and liturgy was donated to the National Cathedral in Washington, D.C.

This lovely carol has been called "the carol of the Reformation." In England in 1855 Catherine Winkworth translated its title as "From Heaven Above to Earth I Come," and some hymnals use her translation. "This little Child, of lowly birth, shall be the joy of all the earth" is a particularly felicitous phrase, as is the reference to "Mary, chosen Mother mild." Miss Winkworth's three-stanza translation is frequently used today.

This chorale is so popular that Johann Sebastian Bach included it in an elaborate style in his *Christmas Oratorio* in 1734, exactly two centuries after Luther composed it for his family gathering.

"FROM HEAVEN HIGH"

From heaven high I come to you,
To bring you tidings strange and true.
Glad tidings of great joy I bring,
Whereof I now will say and sing.

To you this night is born a Child
Of Mary, chosen Mother mild;
This little Child, of lowly birth,
Shall be the joy of all the earth.

Glory to God in highest heaven,
Who unto us His Son hath given!
While angels sing with pious mirth,
A glad New Year to all the earth.

"Good Christian Men, Rejoice"

This carol first appeared in English in John Mason Neale's *Carols for Christmastide* in 1853. It is a translation of a fourteenth-century "macaronic" carol, that is a carol partly in Latin and partly in a vernacular language, such as French, German, or English. In this case, it was a German-Latin carol. Some claim that a fourteenth-century Dominican preacher and mystic, Heinrich Suso, heard these words sung by angels and wrote the tune and lyrics after singing and dancing with them. Suso was a storyteller and poet who led a group called "The Friends of God."

Its title, "In Dulci Jubilo" (Let Songs and Gladness Flow), first appeared in a manuscript at Leipzig University around 1400. A library in Trier, Germany, contains a 1482 manuscript of it. Both Protestants and Catholics in Central Europe loved the carol and included it in their hymnals. In a Moravian missionary diary from Bethlehem, Pennsylvania, an entry for September 14, 1745, recorded that it was a popular song among the faithful and had been translated into many languages.

The carol has gone through many translations and revisions. As several hymnal compilers became concerned about gender-inclusive language during the past two decades, the title was changed to "Good Christian Friends, Rejoice." It is also often sung in Latin.

Herbert Wernecke once wrote, "This song breathes a note of happy Christian fellowship and an abandon of joy that both children and adults feel vividly. The joyous affirmations of Christ's birth inspire a sense of world-wide fellowship uniting all Christians. And the implications of Christ's birth and victory over the grave are themes of joy that move the hearts of men wherever they are sung."

"GOOD CHRISTIAN MEN, REJOICE"

Good Christian men, rejoice
With heart and soul and voice!
Give ye heed to what we say:
News! News!
Jesus Christ is born today!
Ox and ass before Him bow,
And He is in the manger now:
Christ is born today! Christ is born today!

Good Christian men, rejoice
With heart and soul, and voice!
Now ye hear of endless bliss:
Joy! Joy!
Jesus Christ was born for this!
He hath oped the heavenly door,
And man is blessed evermore:
Christ was born for this! Christ was born for this!

Good Christian men, rejoice
With heart and soul, and voice!
Now ye need not fear the grave:
Peace! Peace!
Jesus Christ was born to save!
Calls you one and calls you all,
To gain His everlasting hall:
Christ was born to save! Christ was born to save!

"How Brightly Shines the Morning Star"

This powerful hymn was born out of the turmoil of sixteenth-century Germany, a land wracked by religious and political strife and afflicted by plague and pestilence. Its author was a Lutheran pastor, Philipp Nicolai, who was born in 1556. While he was the pastor of a church in Unna in Westphalia, he witnessed a plague that took thirteen hundred lives. As many as thirty burials a day were conducted in his parish. One day when the tragedy weighed heavily on his heart and soul, he took up his pen and wrote this hymn. It was published in 1599 in his *Meditations on Eternal Life*.

He based his text on Colossians 1:15 and Hebrews 1:1–2 in the New Testament, using references to "Son of God" and "Mary's Son" in his poem. The "Morning Star" terminology comes from Job 38:7 and 2 Peter 1:19.

The hymn became immediately popular and was used as a Christmas offertory hymn and at weddings. It was often chimed from church bell towers, and its words appeared on ornaments. Felix Mendelssohn used it in his oratorio *Christus,* which was based on the life of Christ. Bach borrowed it for one of his compositions, *Cantata no. 1.* Another German composer, Peter Cornelius, used the melody for his carol "The Kings," which remains popular in Germany and England.

Translators have given this song several alternate names. Some hymnbooks call it "How Brightly Beams the Morning Star," after Catherine Winkworth's translation. "How Bright Appears the Morning Star" and "O Morning Star, How Fair and Bright" are other titles.

"HOW BRIGHTLY SHINES THE MORNING STAR"

How brightly shines the morning star,
With mercy beaming from afar;
The host of heav'n rejoices;
O Righteous Branch, O Jesse's Rod!
Thou Son of man and Son of God!
We, too, will lift our voices:
Amen, Amen!
Holy, holy, yet most lowly,
Draw Thou near us;
Great Emmanuel, come and hear us.

Though circled by the hosts on high,
He deigned to cast a pitying eye
Upon His helpless creature;
The whole creation's Head and Lord,
By highest seraphim adored,
Assumed our very nature;

Jesus, grant us,
Through Thy merit, to inherit
Thy salvation;
Hear, O hear our supplication.

Rejoice, ye heavens; thou earth, reply:
With praise, ye sinners, fill the sky,
For this His Incarnation.
Incarnate God, put forth Thy power,
Ride on, ride on, great Conqueror,
Till all know Thy salvation.
Amen, Amen!
Hallelujah! Hallelujah!
Praise be given
Evermore, by earth and heaven.

"Joseph Dearest, Joseph Mine"

This is a German cradlesong that appeared originally in a mystery play, a drama often presented in a cathedral and intended to convey religious messages to a largely unlettered audience. "Joseph Dearest" is very much a children's song. It has an unusual quality since it focuses on Joseph, the foster father of Jesus.

The Oxford Book of Carols says, "This has long been one of the most popular of all Christmas songs in Germany." It is usually sung to a fourteenth-century Latin tune, "Resonet in Laudibus," which was a medieval song sung with the custom of cradle rocking during Christmas services.

British composer Ralph Vaughan Williams did the harmonization for the *English Hymnal* of 1906. In English translations, only a few verses are sung. The original German includes at least eight.

"JOSEPH DEAREST, JOSEPH MINE"

Joseph dearest, Joseph mine,
Help me rock the Child divine;
God reward thee and all that's thine
In paradise, so prays the mother Mary.

Gladly, dear one, lady mine,
I will rock this child of thine;
Heavenly light on us both shall shine
In paradise, as prays the mother Mary.

Peace to all that have good will!
God, who heaven and earth doth fill,
Comes to turn us away from ill,
And lies so still within the crib of Mary.

All shall come and bow the knee;
Wise and happy they shall be,
Loving such a Divinity,
As all may see in Jesus, Son of Mary.

Now is born Emmanuel
As foretold by Ezekiel,
Promised Mary by Gabriel;
Ah! Who can tell thy praises, Son of Mary!

Thou my heart with love hast stirred,
Thou, the Father's eternal Word,
Virtue's shining treasure-hoard,
Who ne'er demurred to be the Son of Mary.

Sweet and lovely little one,
Princely, beauteous, God's own Son,
Without Thee were we all undone:
Our love is won by Thine, O Son of Mary.

Heavenly Child, Thou Lord of all,
Meanly housed in ox's stall,
Free our souls, in Satan's thrall:
On Thee we call, Thou blessed Son of Mary.

"Lo! How a Rose E'er Blooming"

This serenely beautiful and heart-touching carol comes from the Rhineland of Germany, probably from the fifteenth century. It appeared in a collection of folk songs and in a Catholic hymnal in 1599. The music was harmonized by the great German composer Michael Praetorius, himself the author of many Christmas hymns and motets. Praetorius based his setting on a folk tune that appeared in 1536.

The symbolism of a rose blooming "in the cold midwinter and at the midnight hour" is quite effective. (Translations vary: The verse appearing in most hymnals today says, "Amid the cold of winter, when half-spent was the night.") In older hymnals it was called "I Know a

Rose-Tree Springing," but the present title seems both more dramatic and powerful.

The original composition had seventeen stanzas, but only three are generally used in English translations today.

"Lo! How a Rose E'er Blooming"

Lo! how a rose e'er blooming,
From tender stem hath sprung,
Of Jesse's lineage coming
As seers of old have sung;
It came, a blossom bright,
Amid the cold of winter
When half-spent was the night.

Isaiah 'twas foretold it,
The Rose I have in mind;
With Mary we behold it,
The Virgin Mother kind:
To show God's love aright
She bore to us a Savior
When half-spent was the night.

O Flower, whose fragrance tender
With sweetness fills the air,
Dispel in glorious splendor
The darkness everywhere;
True man, yet very God,
From sin and death now save us
And share our every load.

"O Come, Little Children"

This charming nineteenth-century German song is unique in its point of view. It is directed solely at children, imploring them to worship a child like themselves, but a child born to be a King and Savior.

Long popular in Germany, it is known also in its English version. Its author was a German Catholic priest, Christoph von Schmid, who was also a schoolmaster who devoted much of his life to the education and literary uplift of children. Born in 1768, he lived a productive life until his death in 1854. In 1801 he published *Bible Stories for Children*, which retold some of the great and stirring Bible tales at a level that young readers could understand.

His Christmas carol, "O Come, Little Children," was written late in his life, perhaps around 1850. Schmid's poem was set to a melody by Johann Abraham Peter Schulz, a conductor, organist, and composer. Schulz served the king of Denmark for an eight-year tenure, and this tune was probably written during that time. The carol, says musicologist William Studwell, is "quiet, unassuming and totally lacking in pomposity."

"O COME, LITTLE CHILDREN"

O come, little children;
O come one and all,
Who lies in the manger
In Bethlehem's stall;
For there, little children

On this holiest night,
Our God sends from Heaven
His Son, our delight.

He lies there, before you,
Asleep in the hay,
With Mary and Joseph
To guard Him and pray.
The wondering shepherds
Look in at the door,
And seeing the Infant
They kneel and adore.

Adore like the shepherds!
Your glad voices raise
With those of the angels
Who sing in His praise.
Your chorus will echo
From earth to the sky,
With "Glory to God
In His Heaven most high!"

"Silent Night"

This calm and beautiful song is unquestionably the most popular of all Christmas carols in the world. A 1998 poll of the American people placed "Silent Night" far out in front of every other Christmas carol, with 26 percent of Americans—more than seventy million people—citing it as their favorite carol. Recorded versions by Bing Crosby in 1935 and Mahalia Jackson in 1962 were bestsellers.

There is hardly a church in Christendom that doesn't include "Silent Night" on its program. A popular custom in many churches today is to sing this old favorite with electric lights dimmed, lit candles, and the congregation kneeling. It is the signature song of Christmas.

The circumstances surrounding its writing are almost miraculous, the ways in which its popularity grew even more so. While it is fairly well acknowledged that the events occurred in an out-of-the-way place in rural Austria and may have been embellished by the telling or retelling, the basic facts seem reasonably secure. This is because one of the principals, Franz Gruber, wrote a detailed remembrance of how the song was written. Assuming, of course, that his memory was not faulty, we can have a relatively high level of confidence in its facts.

This story begins on Christmas Eve in 1818 in the isolated hamlet of Oberndorf, Austria, a lovely mountainous village eleven miles from Salzburg, the birthplace of the great composer Wolfgang Amadeus Mozart. The village church of St. Nicholas was situated close to the Salzach River, and humidity caused rust to develop in the organ. Finally, just before the Christmas Eve service, the organ broke down. The assistant priest, Father Joseph Mohr, must have dreaded a festive service with no music, so he promptly sat down and wrote a six-stanza poem, "Stille Nacht, Heilige Nacht."

Enter now the part-time organist, Franz Gruber, a local schoolteacher who moonlighted by playing the organ at local churches. In another delightful irony of history, Gruber was supposed to be the organist in the nearby town

of Arnsdorf. But Gruber wanted to double-dip, as it were, so he convinced his stepson to play at Arnsdorf. When Gruber arrived in Oberndorf, Mohr told him of the problem and showed him the poem. Within a few hours Gruber came up with a tune for two solo voices, a chorus, and a guitar. The carol had its premiere in this unlikely midnight setting. We have no record of the audience response, nor do we know how quickly the choir learned the lines. But it is a simple melody.

It might have ended there with a yellowing manuscript, but fate intervened. Next spring an organ repairman, Karl Mauracher, from Zillerthal, Austria, came to fix the rusted organ. Somehow, he emerged with a copy of the song. Returning home, he brought the song to the attention of local singing groups throughout the Tyrol region of Austria, a land where the sound of music was heard regularly throughout the mountains.

Two singing families, the Rainers and the Strassers, added the song to their repertoires. Singing groups were a popular feature of life throughout Germany, Austria, and Central Europe, and people came from far and near to hear the folk music and popular songs of the regions. Country fairs and festivals vied with each other to present the most authentic and vibrant singing groups.

The Strassers performed the carol in Leipzig in 1831 and before the king of Prussia three years later. The king loved it and gave it his endorsement. Sometimes called "The Song of Heaven" or "The Song of Christmas Eve," it appeared in a German song book collection in 1838. It was called a Tyrolean folk song. No one seemed to know the name of the author or the musician. Copyright laws were generally unknown or unenforced, and music was routinely pirated in those days. In 1854 someone in the royal chapel in Berlin wrote to the cathedral church of St. Peter in Salzburg, requesting information about the song. Gruber's son Felix sang in the cathedral choir. He relayed the request to his father, who wrote a detailed history of the song's origin. Gruber, in the intervening years, had become organist and choirmaster at Hallein from 1833 until his death in 1863.

An English language version may have appeared in England in 1849. Emily Elliott, who wrote "Thou Didst Leave Thy Throne," published a translation in 1858 for a church in Brighton, England.

Meanwhile, in America "Silent Night" was soon to be introduced. John Freeman Young translated the carol into English. Young, who was born in 1820 in the farm town of Pittston, Maine, abandoned a scientific career in his mid-twenties and studied for the ministry of the Episcopal Church. Graduating from the Virginia Seminary in Alexandria in 1845, he was assigned to St. John's Church in Jacksonville, Florida. After later serving as a missionary in Texas and Louisiana, he was transferred to New York City's Trinity Church on Wall Street, where the musical program was unsurpassed. It was here that he began to collect many Latin, Greek, and German hymns with the intention of publishing a volume of all the greatest Christian hymns of every age and nation. His translation of "Silent Night" was done in 1863. While trying to complete his hymnal, he was unexpectedly named the Bishop of Florida in 1867.

Returning to Florida, Young worked tirelessly for the next eighteen years and even did some missionary work in Cuba. He died on a business trip to New York in 1885, but shortly before his death he asked his friend Bishop John Henry Hopkins of Vermont (whose son wrote "We Three Kings of Orient Are") to see that his hymn collection was published. It appeared two years later under the title *Great Hymns of the Church*.

Young's translation of "Silent Night" has become the standard for the United States. It is also believed by some scholars that Young added a fourth stanza, which mentions a "wondrous star," since there is no mention of a star in copies of Father Mohr's work.

"The Song of Heaven" has been translated into virtually every language. It was broadcast over Austrian radio every Christmas Eve until the Nazi invasion of 1938, when it was deemed "inappropriate" by the new Nazi government.

Music historian William Studwell says that "Silent Night" is "devout in tone but not weighed down by theological trappings" and thus "embodies the spirit of the holiday more than any other musical piece ever created." Gruber and Mohr probably had no idea what their last-minute, spontaneous efforts had created. But both are immortalized today at the Silent Night Chapel and Museum in the still placid and sparkling village of Oberndorf.

There is a bittersweet quality to Father Mohr's story. The child of a single mother, he remained an obscure parish priest for his entire life. He was transferred from parish to parish and died forgotten and unknown in 1848 at age fifty-six. But his gentle, faith-affirming lyrics will live on until the end of time.

"SILENT NIGHT"

Silent night, holy night,
All is calm, all is bright;
Round yon Virgin, Mother and Child!
Holy Infant, so tender and mild,

Sleep in heavenly peace,
Sleep in heavenly peace.

Silent night, holy night,
Shepherds quake at the sight.
Glories stream from heaven afar
Heavenly hosts sing Alleluia,
Christ the Savior is born!
Christ the Savior is born.

Silent night, holy night!
Son of God, love's pure light.
Radiant beams from Thy holy face
With the dawn of redeeming grace,
Jesus Lord, at Thy birth.
Jesus Lord, at Thy birth.

Silent night, holy night,
Wondrous Star, lend thy light;
With the angels let us sing,
Alleluia to our King;
Christ the Savior is born,
Christ the Savior is born.

V

GREEK AND LATIN
SONGS AND HYMNS

Singing has been a central part of the worship life of Christian communities from the earliest times. References to "psalms, hymns, and spiritual songs" are found in Paul's epistles in the New Testament. These were most likely the psalms of David, with which Jewish followers of Christ would have been familiar. Soon, distinctive hymns and chants were developed, particularly the canticles, or short hymns of praise, found in Luke's Gospel.

Many of these had a direct relationship to the Christmas story. Two of them are Mary's song of praise at the Annunciation, called the Magnificat, and the prayer of the aged Simeon as he held the Christ child in the Temple forty days after the Nativity, called the Nunc Dimittis. The Hebrew Scriptures were adapted for use in the early Christian liturgies. Scholars also suggest that numerous fragments of early hymns or chants can be found in several New Testament passages (1 Timothy 3:16; 2 Timothy 2:11; Ephesians 5:14; James 1:17; and Revelation 1:5–7).

Ignatius of Antioch, a church father and author who was martyred early in the second century, encouraged responsive singing in his congregation. A reference to Christian hymn singing is also found in a letter by Pliny, governor of Bithnia and Pontus, to the Roman emperor Trajan in the year 112. Pliny reported that he heard of "Christians singing songs to Christ, addressing him as God."

In his study *Christ in the Early Christian Hymns*, Daniel Liderbach writes, "The early hymns praised Christ as Savior, Redeemer, the Son of God and the pinnacle of humanity....The earliest Christian hymns confessed an imaginative, Christian faith in Jesus as Lord."

Liderbach argues that most of the earliest Christian hymns dealt with broad themes and categories and did not yet choose to focus on the Nativity or on the human circumstances surrounding the Incarnation. He says, "The earliest Christian hymns confess a faith in the identity of Jesus as the Proclaimer who redeemed, saved, revealed and uplifted. Jesus was the source and cause of human hope. He assured humanity that all sins have been forgiven."

After several church councils in the fourth and fifth centuries set about to define church doctrine, worship itself became more philosophical, and several hymns were written to celebrate the newly established feasts of Christmas and Epiphany. As Christianity emerged from three centuries of persecution, church leaders set about the refinement of worship. Hymns were written mostly in Greek or Syriac, but changed to Latin in the late fourth century in the Western Roman Empire. Some of the church's greatest fathers and saints were noted for their hymns, Clement of Alexandria and St. Ephraem of Edessa, Syria, among them. E. E. Ryden wrote of this era, "Greek hymnody is nearly always objective. It does not concern itself very often with the response of the human soul to the message of the Gospel. As pure worship, Greek hymnody has never been surpassed."

An eighth-century Greek hymn, written by Cosmas of Jerusalem and sung at the Christmas morning service, expresses the sense of joy and triumph felt by Christians of that era. The first verse follows:

> *Christ is born, tell forth His fame!*
> *Christ from heaven, His love proclaim:*
> *Christ on earth, exalt His name.*
> *Sing to the Lord, O world, with exultation;*
> *Break forth in glad thanksgiving, every nation.*
> *For He hath triumphed gloriously!*

"A Christmas Hymn" by St. Romanos the Singer, who was born in Syria, became a deacon in a church in Beirut and then a priest and choirmaster in Constantinople, conveys the Greek understanding of Christmas. It is twenty-five stanzas long, and this is the first stanza:

> *The Virgin this day gives birth*
> *To One beyond all nature.*
> *And Earth draws in, offering a cave*

To One who cannot be approached.
Angels with shepherds give glory
And Magi make their way,
By following after a star;
For there is born to us
A tiny child
Who is God before all times began.

An eighth-century hymn by Andrew of Jerusalem opens with these stirring words:

The righteous rejoice
The heavens are glad,
The mountains leap for joy,
For Christ is born.

In the Western world, Latin hymnody enriched the faithful. St. Hilary of Poitiers, France, wrote the first Latin hymns, but few have survived. St. Ambrose of Milan is called the "father of Latin hymnody." His hymns spread throughout the Christian world and may have played a role in the conversion of the great church father, St. Augustine. In his classic *Confessions*, Augustine described how he felt when he heard the hymns of Ambrose sung in the basilica at Milan: "I wept at the beauty of thy hymns and canticles, and was powerfully moved at the sweet sound of thy church's singing. Those sounds flowed into my ears, and the truth streamed into my heart."

Daniel Joseph Donahue was one of the great scholars of church music, though he was a judge, not a musician or a theologian. His 1908 book *Early Christian Hymns* gives graceful translations from the original Latin. Of Ambrose, he wrote, "St. Ambrose is unquestionably the greatest of all Latin hymn writers. He established the custom of chanting, by alternate choirs, the psalms and other religious songs, in his church at Milan, and this custom soon spread to all churches of the west."

A fifth-century poet, Sedulius, wrote an Epiphany hymn, "Crudelis Herodes, Deum," which asks the question, "Why fear the coming of the King, O cruel Herod?" Sedulius refers to Jesus as the "Celestial Lamb," who "comes to bear our sins, and wash our guilt away, that we with thee, God's love may share." Sedulius retells the story of the wise men in a verse tinged with poetry and mystery:

> *The Magi, follow through the night*
> *The mystic star that goes before;*
> *By light, they seek the Lord of Light,*
> *The King and God whom they adore.*

These Latin hymns have a unique character. Francis X. Weiser reminds us, "The early Latin hymns are profound and solemn, and dwell exclusively on the supernatural aspects of Christmas. Theological in text, they do not concern themselves with the human side of the Nativity." One final selection from the Latin tradition reveals this:

A virgin's womb becomes the shrine
That holds the Lord of heaven and earth,
Through stainless maid, by grace divine,
the God-child hath His wondrous birth.

The stories of five great Greek and Latin hymns that are a part of our modern Christmas celebrations make up this section.

"Earth Has Many a Noble City"

"Earth Has Many a Noble City" is an early Latin Epiphany hymn written by Aurelius Prudentius, the Spanish Christian poet whose late-in-life conversion produced an enormous output of literary material celebrating his new-found faith.

Prudentius celebrates Bethlehem as the noblest city, because out of it "the Lord from heaven came to rule." Rich in symbolism is this lovely verse: "Fairer than the sun at morning was the star that told his birth."

The third and fourth stanzas celebrate the gift of the Magi, whom he calls "Eastern sages" who brought "oblations rich and rare" because of their "deep devotion." He calls their offerings to the young child "sacred gifts of mystic meanings" and then reveals the symbolic meaning of each gift.

The translation used today is by Edward Caswall, a nineteenth-century Englishman who served both the Anglican and Roman Catholic Churches as a clergyman, and who wrote and translated many hymns. He published this hymn in his 1849 book *Lyra Catholica*.

The music is by Christian Friedrich Witt, a German. The tune used is generally the same one as for "Come, Thou Long-Expected Jesus."

"EARTH HAS MANY A NOBLE CITY"

Earth has many a noble city;
Bethlehem, thou dost all excel:
Out of thee the Lord from heaven
Came to rule His Israel.

Fairer than the sun at morning
Was the star that told His birth,
To the world its God announcing
Seen in fleshly form on earth.

Eastern sages at His cradle
Make oblations rich and rare;
See them give, in deep devotion,
Gold, and frankincense, and myrrh.

Sacred gifts of mystic meanings:
Incense doth their God disclose,
God the King of kings proclaimeth,
Myrrh His sepulcher foreshows.

Jesus, whom the Gentiles worshiped
At Thy glad epiphany,
Unto Thee, with God the Father
And the Spirit, glory be.

"O Come, All Ye Faithful"

O Come, All Ye Faithful has such a triumphant, call-to-worship quality about it that it is frequently used as a processional hymn on Christmas Eve. Simple and direct in language and immensely appealing, it ranks sixth in a 1998 survey of Americans' favorite Christmas carols.

Its history has been clothed in mystery, but most music historians are in general agreement of how this majestic hymn emerged as a favorite of worshipers the world over. To this day no one knows for sure who wrote the words. They have been attributed to St. Bonaventure, an anonymous monk in the Cistercian Order, and a French poet who lived in the 1680s.

We do know that the first "copyist," or the one who discovered the original Latin text, "Adeste Fidelis," was John Francis Wade, an English Catholic from Lancashire who spent most of his adult years in Douay, France, a center of English Roman Catholic exiles where the Douay version, the primary English Catholic text of the Bible, was translated. Wade copied music manuscripts and gave music lessons to children of the families residing in Douay. When anti–Roman Catholic legislation and persecution were enforced in England as a result of the "Glorious Revolution" and the Penal Laws, many Roman Catholics settled in this French city. Ironically, the anticlerical and antireligious excesses of the French Revolution drove the English Catholic colony and their French Jesuit allies back to England.

A second copyist was Samuel Webbe, a workaholic cabinetmaker and music copyist. He often worked from five in the morning until midnight. He taught himself languages and became an organist and composer in his own right. "O Come, All Ye Faithful" first appeared in his 1782 book *Essay on Church Plain Chant.* For years the hymn was associated with the chapel of the Portuguese Embassy in London, which is why it was often called the Portuguese hymn. Webbe played the organ at the chapel.

The first English translation was completed by the Reverend Frederick Oakeley, an Oxford graduate who was ordained in the Church of England in 1826. He became rector of the Margaret Street Chapel in 1839 and helped to transform that parish into a renowned center of Anglo-Catholic worship known as All Saints Church. The church was noted for its glorious music and attracted King Edward VII to worship there. Oakeley's translation is substantially the one now familiar to most English-speaking Christians. In 1845 Oakeley chose to become a Roman Catholic, in the same year that John Henry Newman was received. He was ordained to the priesthood in his new faith, becoming a canon at Westminster Cathedral and living what one biographer called "an uneventful but exemplary life serving the poor." In 1852 this increasingly popular hymn appeared in F. H. Murray's *A Hymnal for Use in the English Church.*

Modern scholars now believe that Wade himself wrote the hymn rather than merely "copying" or translating it. In 1946 a manuscript acquired by hymnologist

Maurice Frost, vicar of the parish church of Reddington in Oxfordshire, England, strongly suggested Wade's authorship. A scholarly monk, Dom John Stephan, concurred in a 1947 monograph. But he only wrote the first five of the eight original stanzas, so a mystery remains. Scholars now believe that a French abbe, Etienne Borderies, who fled Revolutionary France for England in 1793, wrote the three concluding Latin stanzas. These three verses are rarely sung today (another Anglican clergyman, William Mercer, may have written the fourth and fifth stanzas, just to add to the confusion). The convoluted history of this carol shows how some of our beloved hymns have been altered, revised, and sometimes just mysteriously appeared in hymnbooks and song books without attribution.

The stanzas sung today include an invitation for believers to come to Bethlehem, an affirmation of faith in the second stanza, an exhortation to worship in the third, and a salutation to the newborn King in the fourth.

Of this hymn Canon Frank Colquhoun, once dean of Norwich Cathedral, wrote, "With hearts full of wonder and gratitude, we greet our Lord and give glory to him as the incarnate Word of the Father. The Incarnation is not simply a piece of religious dogma. It is a theme for exultant song." William J. Reynolds adds, "Here is a joyous song of adoration of Christ. It is a simple expression, folklike in character, and cherished by Christians everywhere."

"O COME ALL YE FAITHFUL"

O come, all ye faithful, joyful and triumphant,
O come ye, O come ye to Bethlehem!
Come and behold Him, born the King of angels!

Refrain:

O come, let us adore Him,
O come, let us adore Him,
O come, let us adore Him,
Christ, the Lord!

God of God, Light of Light,
Lo, He abhors not the Virgin's womb;
Very God, begotten, not created:

See how the shepherds, summoned to His cradle,
Leaving their flocks, draw nigh to gaze;
We too will thither, bend our joyful footsteps:

Lo, star-led chieftains, Magi, Christ adoring,
Offer Him incense, gold, and myrrh;
We to the Christ-child, bring our hearts' oblations:

Child, for us sinners, poor and in the manger,
Fain we embrace Thee, with love and awe;
Who would not love Thee, loving us so dearly?

Sing, choirs of angels, sing in exultation,
O sing, all ye citizens of heav'n above!
Glory to God, all glory in the highest!

Yea, Lord, we greet Thee, born this happy morning,
Jesus, to Thee be all glory giv'n;
Word of the Father, now in flesh appearing!

"O Come, O Come, Emmanuel"

"O Come, O Come, Emmanuel" is a splendid example of medieval plainsong or plainchant formerly associated with monasteries. It is sung during the Advent season, that four-week period of penitence and preparation that precedes Christmas and has been part of the church calendar in the West since the sixth or seventh centuries. In the East, Advent began even earlier and is longer in duration. "O Come, O Come, Emmanuel" is often a processional hymn on Sundays in Advent, but it can be heard all during the Advent and Christmas seasons.

Several elements in this carol are almost unique to the season. By the eighth or ninth centuries, the Roman liturgy included a series of antiphons, short scriptural hymns, at Vespers during Advent. They were collectively called the "O Antiphons" because the first word was O as in O wisdom, O Lord of Hosts, O Root of Jesse, and so on. These songs are mostly Old Testament prophecies that found fulfillment in the coming of Christ. The imagery is rich and recalls ancient times.

These antiphons, sung at Vespers from December 17 to December 23, retained their popularity in the Church of England after the Reformation and are now sung in many traditions. This particular hymn setting may date from the twelfth century when an unknown poet selected five of the seven Advent antiphons and turned them into a Latin hymn. As such, the final product is, as Canon Colquhoun observes, "a fivefold portrait of Christ who is seen as the Incarnate Word, the Son of David, the Light of the world, the Key to heaven's door, the Lord of might." *Emmanuel* is a Hebrew word meaning "God with us" (see Isaiah 8:8; Matthew 1:22–23).

The form of the hymn best known today is largely from the brilliant pen of translator John Mason Neale. Neale is a figure who appears throughout this book because his translations of ancient Latin and Greek carols have immeasurably enriched the worship experiences of countless English-speaking Christians for a century and a half. Neale, a scholarly priest of the Church of England, produced more than a dozen volumes of hymns and carols in forty-eight short years (1818–66). Most were translated from classic Latin and Greek sources, but Neale also read Danish, Swedish, and a number of other languages. His 1853 *Carols for Christmas Tide* includes most of his translations and some original carols.

Neale's prodigious research took him to the Eastern Christian world, where he developed a profound admiration for Eastern Orthodox Christianity, especially its ethereal liturgy. His two-volume *History of the Holy Eastern Church* was his personal favorite among his literary accomplishments. For this work he received a personal gift of a treasured manuscript from the Metropolitan of Russia, one of the leaders of the Russian Orthodox Church.

A graduate of Cambridge University in his native England, he received no honors in his homeland. In the United States, Harvard University and Trinity College in Hartford bestowed honorary doctorates on Neale.

A group of musicologists who put together the *Episcopal Hymnal* of 1940 had this to say of Neale: "His character was a happy mixture of gentleness and firmness, with an unbounded charity which, with his liturgical studies and literary attainments, won him a world-wide love and respect."

"O Come, O Come, Emmanuel" has become a worthy addition to the Advent-Christmas season. Ernest Emurian celebrated it: "'O Come, O Come Emmanuel,' with its dignity and restraint, its majesty and stateliness, continues to add its poignant musical ministry to the true spirit of the season, bringing with it a tie that extends back beyond the Middle Ages, reminding believers of every age that the news of the birth of the Son of God is always an occasion for merriment and mirth, and will always inspire rejoicing and singing."

"O Come, O Come, Emmanuel"

O Come, O come, Emmanuel,
And ransom captive Israel,
That mourns in lonely exile here
Until the Son of God appear.

Refrain:

Rejoice! Rejoice! Emmanuel
Shall come to thee, O Israel!

O come, O come, Thou Rod of Jesse, free
Thine own from Satan's tyranny;
From depths of hell Thy people save,
And give them victory o'er the grave.

O come, Thou Dayspring, come and cheer
Our spirits by Thine advent here;
Disperse the gloomy clouds of night,
And death's dark shadows put to flight.

O come, Thou Key of David, come,
And open wide our heav'nly home;
Make safe the way that leads on high,
And close the path to misery.

O come, O come, Thou Lord of might,
Who once, from Sinai's flaming height
Didst give the trembling tribes Thy law,
In cloud, and majesty, and awe.

"O Gladsome Light"

This hymn, often called the "Greek Candlelighting Hymn," is one of the most ancient Christian songs and may even have appeared in the second century. It was not intended as a Christmas hymn but rather as a hymn for

evening worship, which would have required candles to provide light. It has been ascribed to Sophronius and was quoted by St. Basil in the fourth century.

While not intended for Christmas, it is often a part of the Christmas worship experiences. More often it is sung on Candlemas Day, February 2, which is regarded by some historians of worship and liturgy as the true ending of the Christmas-Epiphany season. Candlemas, which includes the blessing of candles, is also the Feast of the Purification of the Blessed Virgin Mary and the Presentation of Christ in the Temple, the official though lengthy name. It commemorates the Jewish requirement that a mother must be ritually purified in the Temple forty days afer childbirth. In the New Testament this event is recorded and is included in the story of Simeon, who, after seeing the child Jesus, exclaimed, "Lord lettest now thy servant depart in peace for mine eyes have seen my salvation," a canticle appointed to the Evensong liturgy in the Anglican churches of the world (called the Nunc Dimittis).

John Keble, a nineteenth-century English clergyman and leader of the Oxford Movement for the revitalization of the Church of England, translated this hymn as "Hail, Gladdening Light," and this title is often found in hymnals today.

To further confuse the matter, this hymn sometimes appears as "O Brightness of the Immortal Father's Face." Another translation by Robert Bridges, an English poet born in 1844, is called "O Gladsome Light." Henry Wadsworth Longfellow also loved this ancient Greek hymn and included it in his *Golden Legend*.

Canon Peter Harvey, an English pastor who loved hymns and their stories, said, "The Candlelighting Hymn of so long ago speaks to us most eloquently of the faith which alone can dispel the gloom and darkness of a troubled world."

"O GLADSOME LIGHT"

O gladsome light, O grace
Of God the Father's face,
The eternal splendor wearing;
Celestial, holy, blest,
Our Savior Jesus Christ,
Joyful in thine appearing.

Now, ere day fadeth quite,
We see the evening light,
Our wonted hymn outpouring;
Father of might unknown,
Thee, His incarnate Son,
And Holy Spirit adoring.

To Thee of right belongs
All praise of holy songs,
O Son of God, Lifegiver;
Thee, therefore, O Most High,
The world doth glorify,
And shall exalt forever.

"Of the Father's Love Begotten"

This theologically profound and faith-affirming hymn is a candidate for the first Christmas hymn ever written. It appears sometime in the late fourth or early fifth century in a long sacred poem, the *Cathemerinon*, written by Marcus Aurelius Clemens Prudentius.

Prudentius was a lawyer and magistrate in Spain during the Roman Empire's latter days. His father was not a Christian but an admirer of the Roman emperor and stoic philosopher Marcus Aurelius, for whom he named his son. The son, however, became a convinced and committed Christian late in life. He wrote a number of books that were widely read in the Middle Ages. His writings were so voluminous that he was called "The Christian Pindar," after the Roman poet. The Medieval Academy of America published a concordance of his works in 1932, suggesting that his highly personal musings on faith were still being read more than fifteen hundred years after his death in 410. His poems became hymns and were used in church rites and festivals for centuries.

Ian Bradley calls this wonderful hymn of the ancient church "a fine processional hymn which speaks so majestically and sonorously about Christ in all his attributes, human and divine." Popular throughout all of history, it blossomed again in the ninth century and was sung in Spain throughout the Christmas season, including the Feast of the Circumcision on January 1. At York Cathedral in England it was sung at the evening services called compline from Christmas Eve until Epiphany. Bradley adds, "It is not surprising that when the Oxford Movement prompted a revival of the early office hymns of the church, this comprehensive and well-written treatment of the Christmas message in all its theological complexity was one of the first texts to be translated and brought into use in the mid-Victorian Church of England."

The best-known translation of "Of the Father's Love" was made by John Mason Neale in 1851. The music generally used is plainsong chant from the Middle Ages. Not all of the ten verses are usually sung. Often only one or two will suffice to convey the meaning of the incarnation of the Son of God, "who was begotten not made, being of one substance with the Father by whom all things were made." Some translations call this "Of the Father's Heart Begotten," but Neale's translation of love has remained the most popular.

Whether sung in a grand cathedral with organ and choir, or by a solo singer on a dulcimer, it remains a quite extraordinary reflection on what really happened that night in Bethlehem.

"OF THE FATHER'S LOVE BEGOTTEN"

Of the Father's love begotten
Ere the worlds began to be,
He is Alpha and Omega,
He the Source, the Ending He.
Of the things that are, that have been,
And that future years shall see,
Evermore and evermore.

O that birth for ever blessed,
When the Virgin, full of grace,
By the Holy Ghost conceiving,

Bore the Savior of our race;
And the Babe, the world's Redeemer
First revealed His sacred face,
Evermore and evermore!

O ye heights of heaven adore Him;
Angel hosts, His praises sing;
Powers, dominions, bow before Him,
And extol our God and King;
Let no tongue on earth be silent,
Every voice in concert ring,
Evermore and evermore!

Christ, to thee with God the Father,
And, O Holy Ghost, to Thee,
Hymn and chant and high thanksgiving,
And unwearied praises be:
Honor, glory, and dominion,
And eternal victory,
Evermore and evermore!

VI

A CLASSICAL CHRISTMAS

In this section we include some of the wonderful oratorios, cantatas, and other types of sacred choral music that are likely to appear on concert programs or in church celebrations at the Christmas season. They have been selected for their rich and enduring spiritual themes and for their contributions to the joy of Christmas. There are, of course, many others that could have been included here, but these are, we feel, the best.

At its most basic, the oratorio can be defined as sacred opera. Annie Patterson called it "the highest art form by means of which music can be made the vehicle of religious thought" and compared it to a cathedral. Combining many elements of medieval mystery and miracle plays with the sacred musical dramas developed in sixteenth-century Italy by St. Philip Neri, the oratorio's first appearance was in February 1600, in the Church of St. Maria Vallicella in Rome. Emilio del Cavaliere's *L'Anima ed il Corpo* inaugurated what soon became a highlight of the music season throughout

Europe. Bach, Handel, Haydn, Beethoven, Schutz, Mendelssohn, Gounod, and many other composers added to the history of the oratorio. Almost all were based on biblical themes, and both Protestants and Catholics flocked to the performances. Several important oratorios have Christmas themes.

Handel's *Messiah*

If any piece of music signifies the grandeur of a classical Christmas, it is the extraordinary composition called *Messiah* by the German composer George Frideric Handel. Handel wrote all kinds of choral, orchestral, instrumental, and organ music both in Germany and in England, where he settled. He soon became an acknowledged master of the oratorio, composing such works as *Esther* and *Israel in Egypt.*

Handel began work on the *Messiah* on August 22, 1741, and completed it on the fourteenth of September that year. It must have been a feverish production, as Handel saw this as his masterpiece, a musical retelling of the life of Christ, from birth to resurrection. Handel was apparently seized with a genuine religious fervor during his writing and composition, a realization that this was something that would outlive him and would have the potential of reaching a wide audience with a spiritual message. Handel's biographers are in complete agreement that the *Messiah* represented a culmination of Handel's spirituality and musical talents. Handel himself wrote later, "I did think I did see all heaven before me, and the good God himself."

The premiere of the *Messiah* was held in Ireland's capital city of Dublin. The reasons are several. The Lord Lieutenant, a patron of Handel, invited him to Ireland. Handel's friend, the violinist Matthew Dubourg, lived in Dublin. Three charitable institutions in Ireland were to benefit from the performance. And, finally, a new "Great Music Hall" had just opened on Fishamble Street, near the docks of the River Liffey.

The time was thus propitious for an extraordinary event. Handel had started his journey to Dublin in November 1741. Bad weather caused him to delay at Chester, where he tried out several of his selections with a local choir. Finally arriving in Ireland, Handel polished his work, and occasionally gave a series of concerts at the new Fishamble Street Musick Hall.

A rehearsal of *Messiah* was scheduled for April 8, 1742, at the Music Hall. The enthusiasm was infectious. *Faulkner's Journal,* a leading newspaper of the day, called it "the finest composition of musick that ever was heard," and the *Dublin News Letter* said, "Mr. Handel's new sacred oratorio far surpasses anything of that nature, which has been performed in this or any other kingdom."

The first official performance was scheduled for Monday, April 12, but was postponed until Tuesday, April 13, to accommodate "several persons of distinction." Handel played the organ, and the male choirs of both of Dublin's great cathedrals, Christ Church and St. Patrick's, sang the arias and choruses. Two hospitals and the prisoners in several jails were the intended beneficiaries of this charitable performance.

News from the rehearsal performance the previous week changed the character of the premiere from a gala extravaganza to a more solemn religious experience. On the morning of the performance, a notice in *Faulkner's Journal* asked that the ladies not wear their hoops and requested that "gentlemen come without their swords." The next day's edition praised the composition, saying, "Words are wanting to express the exquisite delight afforded to the admiring crowded audience."

An encore performance was heard on June 3. Handel sent his thanks to the Irish people, whom he called "that generous and polite nation."

The *Messiah* was given its London premiere on March 23, 1743, during which King George II rose to his feet during the singing of the "Hallelujah" chorus, inaugurating a custom that has endured to this day.

Annie Patterson, writing in the florid style of the early twentieth century, praised the *Messiah's* long-range influence on music history. She wrote, "It appeals to men and women of all classes and grades of social and intellectual standing; it furnishes the most appropriate and impressive Christmas and Easter sacred music; it is a standard work for musical societies and choral organizations; it supplies unsurpassable and indispensable items for the repertories of all singers; lastly, as moral elevator and spiritual comforter, the *Messiah* wields a power that is immeasurable."

The *Messiah* was first heard in the U.S. on January 16, 1770, in the music room of the New York City Tavern, of all places! Selections from the oratorio were included in a sacred music concert performed to honor William Tuckey, the longtime choirmaster of Trinity Episcopal Church on Wall Street. In October of that year, portions of *Messiah* were given at Trinity Church. It was not until Christmas Day in 1818 that the entire *Messiah* was presented to an American audience, this time at Boston's Boylston Hall under the auspices of the Handel and Haydn Society. Thirteen years later, New Yorkers heard the entire oratorio at St. Paul's Chapel. From that time until the present, cities large and small have ushered in the Christmas season by presenting at least the Christmas section of the Handel masterpiece.

Handel was a musical genius and a complex personality. A lifelong bachelor, he was strongly opinionated and given to great acts of charity. A sincerely religious man, he saw his oratorios and religious works as extensions of his inner character and as offerings to God. In his book *The Spiritual Lives of Great Composers*, Patrick Kavanagh wrote of him, "He was a relentless optimist whose faith in God sustained him through every difficulty. Raised a sincere Lutheran, he harbored no sectarian animosity and steered clear of denominational disagreements."

Handel threw himself into a composition he called simply *Messiah* because it was an attempt to summarize the life and work of Christ in the musical form that

Handel knew and loved. The entire work of fifty individual selections took only twenty-four days of intense work to accomplish; he rarely left his rooms, working night and day. What emerged was not just a series of vignettes of Christ's life but "a representation of the fulfillment of Redemption through the Redeemer," wrote Handel biographer Jens Peter Larsen.

The Christmas portion of *Messiah* is only a section of Part 1 but includes wonderful orchestral music to set the tone, and arias and recitatives of great joy and happiness. The Christmas section includes Old Testament prophecies and then moves effortlessly into the Nativity narrative. "For Unto Us" is an audience favorite, described by Melvin Berger as "a rapturous choral announcement of the birth of Jesus."

Handel, who visited Italy and in fact lived there for several years, may have borrowed some melodies from the "Pifferari," bagpipe-playing shepherds and troubadours who came from the mountains to serenade residents of Rome and Naples at Christmastime. His Pastoral Symphony section evokes the Christmas folk songs of Italy. The Christmas section ends with "Glory to God," a hymn of praise.

When Handel conducted performances of *Messiah* during his lifetime, he preferred the Easter season and generally sought to present the entire oratorio. He tended to use a small choir and larger orchestra. Today's *Messiah* performances tend to be grand affairs, with huge choirs. The "Hallelujah Chorus" is usually sung at Christmas performances, even though it is a paen to the Resurrection. But audiences love it and demand it at all times.

Berger writes that Handel's *Messiah* "unquestionably holds the position of the most frequently performed choral masterpiece." There is hardly a town in the United States or any other English-speaking country that does not offer at least one Christmas performance of Handel's immortal masterpiece.

Handel died in London on April 14—Holy Saturday, the eve of Easter, as he had wished—in 1759. Thousands attended his funeral. He is buried in Westminster Abbey, where a statue near his grave shows him holding a manuscript. Appropriately, it is "I Know That My Redeemer Liveth" from *Messiah*.

The *Messiah's* impact on the appeal of religious music has been profound and far-reaching. But the impact of the composition personally was also a reflection of a newfound spirituality. Robert Turnbull, who studied the influence of religious belief on artistic temperament, observed, "Handel is the popular preacher of music. Religion would always touch him on his emotional side, and in his later years he seems to have taken seriously to church-going. For the last two or three years of his life, he was used to attend divine service in his own parish church of St. George, Hanover Square, where he was seen on his knees, expressing the utmost fervor of devotion."

Amazingly enough, *Messiah* was criticized by some churchmen, including John Newton, author of "Amazing Grace," for being too secular! Handel did, of course, borrow some of his secular melodies for use in a sacred work, but he saw no problem with that.

Annie Patterson, writing nearly a century ago, called it "the greatest oratorio every penned." She added, "It is a work for all time and for all men. Were all musical masterpieces, save one, doomed to destruction, perhaps that most salutary for preservation would be Handel's great oratorio, *Messiah*."

Bach's *Christmas Oratorio*

Bach's *Christmas Oratorio* actually consists of six cantatas—shorter sacred songs—for Christmas, Epiphany, and the Festival of the Circumcision, which for centuries occurred on January 1. Johann Sebastian Bach spent a great period of his life as choir director, or cantor, to some of the major Lutheran churches in Germany, mainly in Leipzig. He was required not only to direct the choir and arrange the musical portions of the worship service but also to create original compositions.

A cantata (normally a half-hour in length) included choruses and chorales, which Luther and his progeny had contributed to the musical culture of the German Reformation. Stirring, profound, and solemn, these chorales still move worshipers today. Often meditative and subjective, they offer an opportunity for introspection on the part of singers and worshipers alike. Between 1723 and 1744 Bach composed 265 cantatas.

The opening chorus sets the tone of the *Christmas Oratorio*:

> *Christians, be joyful, and praise your salvation,*
> *Sing, for today your Redeemer is born.*
> *Cease to be fearful, forget lamentation,*
> *Haste with thanksgiving to greet this glad morn!*
> *Come, let us worship, and fall down before Him,*
> *Let us with voices united adore Him.*

A tenor sings the familiar words of Holy Scripture, followed by a kind of commentary or aside on the events applying the meaning of the ancient story to the hearer. Interspersed between chorales are more readings of Scripture and additional commentaries that illuminate the text and guide the listener toward belief. The concluding chorale for the first day goes like this:

> *Ah! dearest Jesus, Holy Child,*
> *Make Thee a bed, soft, undefil'd,*
> *Within my heart, and there recline,*
> *And keep that chamber ever Thine.*

The "second day for the festival of Christmas" opens with the shepherds in the field and includes a stirring chorale that may be the best-known selection in the entire oratorio:

> *Break forth, O beauteous heavenly light,*
> *And usher in the morning;*

Ye shepherds, shrink not with affright,
But hear the angel's warning.
This Child, now weak in infancy,
Our confidence and joy shall be,
The power of Satan breaking,
Our peace eternal making.

The entire oratorio is a richly rewarding Christmas experience. Writes Charles Sanford Terry, "Bach's cantatas are not intelligible unless we realize that, when writing them, he placed himself in the pulpit, as it were, to expound the Gospel in the language of his art. To the task he brought a mind versed in theological dialectic, and a devout spirit resolved to clothe his exposition in the most persuasive form of which his art was capable....Throughout his life religion was his staff and comfort. With what vivid literalness he read his Bible is evident in the music with which he clothed its text."

Hector Berlioz's *L'enfance du Christ*

Hector Berlioz's "L'enfance du Christ" (The Infancy of Christ) has an appealing charm and tenderness that has sustained it in the musical repertory since the 1850s. Its most notable section is the chorus of shepherds in the "Flight into Egypt" section, beginning with "Thou must leave thy lovely dwelling, the humble crib, the stable bare." Percy M. Young, an eminent historian of choral music, wrote of this piece, "Berlioz is at his gentlest, his most poetical, and his most self-effacing. Altogether this is an extended pastorale with a dedicated purpose. Berlioz matches Haydn and Handel and Domenico Scarlatti and Corelli in charm and affection. Here, in music, is the sweetness of Fra Angelico."

Berlioz was born in 1803 in an isolated hamlet in rural France near Grenoble. He studied medicine but turned to music after being captivated by the opera. He is best known for his operas *Romeo and Juliet* and *The Damnation of Faust.*

Berlioz's *L'enfance du Christ* premiered on December 10, 1854, at the Salle Herz in Paris, a concert hall rather than a church. In Berlioz's own *Memoirs* he refers to this composition as "soft and tender" and adds this memory from a June 22, 1863, performance in Strasbourg, "To my astonishment, it aroused profound emotion and the unaccompanied mystic chorus at the end drew tears from many."

Berlioz is often thought of as something of a religious skeptic, but he explained in his *Memoirs*, "I need scarcely state that I was brought up as a member of the Holy Catholic and Apostolic Church of Rome. Though we quarreled long ago, I still retain the tenderest recollections of that form of religious belief."

These memories of a childhood faith seem to have influenced this unusual oratorio about the childhood of Christ. The "Shepherd's Chorus" and the lively "Il est ne, le divine enfant," are often included in Christmas musical programs.

Berlioz also wrote the highly praised *Symphonie Fantastique* and a beautiful *Requiem.* He died in Paris in 1869.

Saint Saens's *Christmas Oratorio*

Saint Saens was not noted for his religious music, but this 1854 composition, written early in his career, is an exceptional composition. It is not considered one of the great Christmas oratorios, but it has elements of serene beauty. After a pastoral prelude, the work goes into a chorus, "There were shepherds," a retelling of Luke's narrative. The angelic chorus, "Gloria in Excelsis," follows.

Then Saint Saens turns to a reflective and meditative solo, "Patiently, Patiently Have I Waited for the Lord," and this is followed by a mixed solo and chorus, "In My Heart I Believe," which seems to be a statement of personal faith by a very young man.

Then comes a duet, "Blessed, Blessed Is He Who Cometh," a passage usually associated with Palm Sunday or with the Ordinary of the Mass (the fixed portion of the liturgy). A rather strange and jarring chorus, "Wherefore Do the Heathen Clamor" is followed by two joyous songs, "The Magnificat of the Virgin Mary" and a stirring "Alleluia," which opens:

> *Ye heavens sing praises*
> *Be joyful on earth*
> *For the Lord hath poured His consolation*
> *Upon His people.*

Two final choruses continue the theme of rejoicing.

Saint-Saens wrote *Christmas Oratorio* in Latin. An English translation was published in 1891. Born in Paris in 1835, he was organist at the famed Church of the Madeleine from 1857 to 1876. He wrote masses and motets for the church, but he is probably best known for his opera, *Samson and Delilah,* and his symphonic poem, *Danse Macabre.* A prolific writer, he published volumes of poetry, essays, and studies of astronomy and the natural sciences. An associate of Rossini and Liszt, he died in Algiers in 1921.

Schutz's *Christmas Oratorio*

Heinrich Schutz's *Christmas Oratorio,* written in 1664, is one of the earliest examples of the musical form. Percy Young calls it "the most fascinating, the most joyful and the most charming of all of the works of Schutz." Schutz had also written the *Psalms of David,* the *Resurrection Oratorio,* and *The Seven Last Words,* all of which made him a highly respected composer in seventeenth-century Germany. After studying law at the University of Marburg, he switched to music and became the chief musician, or kapellmeister, at the Royal Court of Dresden. He lived in Copenhagen and Venice at times, but he is most associated with Germany and German choral music. Schutz was seventy-nine years old when he composed *The History of the Joyful and Gracious Birth of Jesus Christ, the Son of God and Mary,* commonly called the *Christmas Oratorio.*

His *Christmas Oratorio* consists of eight scenes, preceded by Luke's Nativity narrative. Angels, shepherds, angelic choruses, wise men, high priests, even King

Herod all appear in various scenes, accompanied by musical instruments (trombones represent the voice of God, for example). The atmosphere conveyed is reverent. Percy Young says, "One may feel the whole work as an extended chorale and as an idealization of a childlike devotion to the fragrance of the Christmas narrative."

Charpentier's Midnight Mass

Marc-Antoine Charpentier's *Midnight Mass* was written in seventeenth-century France at a time when Christmas carols were being interpolated and incorporated into orchestral suites, chamber music, and symphonic music. Charpentier used the structure of the Latin mass to create one of the richest, most melodic, and soaring Christmas pieces in the classical tradition. He used French carols for the six major settings of the Ordinary of the Mass. Such simple pastorals as "Joseph has a good wife" and "Mary, will you tell us" went into the Kyrie, while the Gloria included selections from "Where have the good shepherds gone?" The purely instrumental offertory section is a rendition of "Let your cattle graze."

Charpentier, who studied in Rome under the great Italian oratorio composer Giacomo Carissimi, wrote a Christmas cantata, "Song for the Birth of Our Lord Jesus Christ" (In Nativitatem Domini Nostri Jesu Christi Canticum). This Latin cantata is noted for a solo aria of an angel who announces the holy birth to shepherds in the fields and for its chorus of rejoicing shepherds at the close.

Monteverdi's *Christmas Vespers*

Claudio Monteverdi's *Christmas Vespers* is a triumphant, majestic example of Italian Baroque church music written for the vesper services that Catholic churches celebrated on Sunday evenings for many centuries (and monasteries still do). Monteverdi, like Bach, was the choir director (maestro di cappelle) of a major church, St. Mark's Basilica in Venice, where he was called upon to take charge of all the music and to compose new music. He held this post for thirty years, from 1613 until his death in 1643. He is said to have raised the standard of music to a remarkable degree during his tenure.

The *Christmas Vespers* were usually sung on Christmas Eve, and people came from far and near to experience the richness of soloists, double choir, string orchestra, trombones, and organ. Monteverdi's setting, sung entirely in Latin, consists of Psalms 109, 110, 111, 112, and 116. Interspersed are antiphons ("The King of Peace is highly exalted, for whose countenance all the earth longeth") and supplications ("O God, make speed to save us. O Lord, make haste to help us"). The events of the Nativity are not as central to the narrative as are reflections on the foretelling, the preparation and, then, the meaning of the event for the listener.

Only in the third part does the music take on a Christmas-like character in Monteverdi's setting of the ancient hymn "Christe Redemptor Omnium" and the lovely antiphon "Hodie Christus Natus Est" (Today Christ Is Born). The "Hodie," with its happy countenance of "angels singing, archangels rejoicing," is often heard as a separate piece. Monteverdi concludes his Vespers with his "Magnificat," the song of the Virgin Mary in Luke's Gospel.

German Baroque Cantatas

The late seventeenth and early eighteenth centuries were the golden age of the Baroque era in art and music, a lush, complex, and imaginative time of artistic achievement. Church music, architecture, and painting all reflected this new era. In Germany, composers embellished and enriched the Christmas and Advent celebration in both the Lutheran and Catholic traditions. The "Church Cantatas" were, in particular, a very German and Lutheran contribution to religious music, and no holiday aroused the artistic imagination more than Christmas. Joshua Rifkin wrote, "Perhaps no nation contributed so much to the rich store of Christmas music as did Lutheran Germany."

George Philipp Telemann's "Praise God, Ye Christians All Together" uses biblical verses, Lutheran chorales, and original poetry to create a cantata of great symmetry and beauty. On Christmas Day, Telemann's music concludes, "Once more the door to Paradise is opened." Philipp Erlebach's "Behold, I Bring You Tidings of Great Joy" and Johann Rudolf Ahle's "Take Heed, My Heart" are other notable examples of this art form.

Michael Praetorius, who lived at the transition period from the Renaissance to the Baroque, was an organist and choir director. His five Christmas hymns from "Musae

Sioniae" are settings of Martin Luther's own translations of Latin hymns into German. Praetorius added scoring for a mixed ensemble of voices and instruments to the familiar chorale melodies. "How Brightly Shines the Morning Star" is another of his compositions.

The Danish composer Dietrich Buxtehude's "The Newborn Child," for strings and four voices, is another charming example of the tender cradlesong. Buxtehude's verses were clearly designed to bring hope to listeners, with such phrases as "Little Jesus is our refuge, why should we grieve anymore?"

Latin and English Motets

O Magnum Mysterium (O Great Mystery), a popular motet written for Christmas, highlights the mystery of the Incarnation. Assigned to the morning service (matins) for Christmas Day, it has been set to magnificent music by Alessandro Scarlatti and Giovanni Gabrielli, among others. These Italian Renaissance composers usually required a double choir or two choruses to do their choral works justice.

See, the Word Is Incarnate by England's Orlando Gibbons is an anthem designed for the English church. Gibbons, who is perhaps best known for his grand Palm Sunday anthem, *Hosanna to the Son of David,* wrote ceremonial and choral music in the early seventeenth century. He was organist at the Chapel Royal but died young, at age forty-two, in Canterbury of a stroke on June 5, 1625.

From Virgin's Womb by William Byrd, who lived in England from 1543 until 1623, is a beautiful setting of an old English carol. *This Day Christ Was Born* is a festive anthem setting of *Hodie Christus Natus Est.* Byrd was associated with the Chapel Royal for more than fifty years, writing service music for the Anglican Church in both English and Latin. Byrd remained a Roman Catholic, and his music has been prized by both churches. His Epiphany anthem, *Praise Our Lord, All Ye Gentiles* was a popular Tudor church ceremonial. His masses are still sung, as is his sublime communion motet, *Ave Verum Corpus.*

Cantate Domino, a setting of Psalm 96 appointed for the Christmas morning liturgy, has been a source of numerous musical settings. An eighteenth-century French composer, Jean Joseph de Mondonville, created a particularly rich setting when he was twenty-seven years old. A student of the violin, Mondonville wrote church music for the Royal Chapel at Versailles from 1744 until his death in 1772.

Hodie Christus Natus Est by Jan Sweelinck, an organist and composer of many choral works at the Old Church in Amsterdam, is one of the most upbeat and joyous Christmas motets, filled as it is with the ringing exclamations of alleluia. Its English translation conveys these sentiments:

> *Christ is born today.*
> *On this day the Savior has appeared.*
> *Alleluia.*
> *On this day on earth*
> *The choirs of angels sing rejoicing.*

On this day exultant voices are saying,
Gloria in excelsis deo.
Alleluia.

Britten's "A Ceremony of Carols, op. 28"

Benjamin Britten's "A Ceremony of Carols, op. 28" is a mainstay of the classical Christmas repertory. It was written on a Swedish freighter during the spring of 1942, while Britten was returning to England from the United States in the middle of World War II, no less.

He took for his text nine medieval carols, accompanied by a harp. The processional is the traditional Latin hymn, "Hodie Christus Natus Est," sung a capella. Two Robert Southwell poems, "This Little Babe" and "In Freezing Winter Night," are inspirations for two carols. A version of "There Is No Rose" and a number of cradlesongs and lively carols complete the program.

Britten's low-key, economical style has made this appealing to concertgoers since its premiere in Norwich, England, on December 5, 1942. *The Rough Guide to Classical Music* called this "a simple, tuneful, and inventive celebration of innocence."

Williams's "Fantasia on Christmas Carols"

England's Ralph Vaughan Williams was long influenced in his musical compositions by Christmas carols and the tradition of choral hymns in the church. His 1912 work

"Fantasia on Christmas Carols" for baritone solo, chorus, and orchestra masterfully blends some ancient English carols into the modern musical idiom.

In an autobiographical sketch, Vaughan Williams related that his first contact with English folk songs came with his discovery of Stainer and Bramley's *Christmas Carols, New and Old*, one of the classic carol anthologies. He was especially taken with the "Cherry Tree Carol."

Vaughan Williams composed a ballet, *On Christmas Night,* based on Dickens's *A Christmas Carol.* He wrote a considerable amount of church music, including complete services for Matins, Holy Communion, and Evensong for the Church of England, a Festival "Te Deum," a "Mass in G Minor," motets, variations on Welsh hymns, and a "Thanksgiving for a Victory," blending selections from the Bible, Shakespeare, and Kipling. He was editor of *The English Hymnal,* coeditor of *Songs of Praise,* and coeditor of the magisterial *Oxford Book of Carols.*

SUGGESTIONS FOR
FURTHER READING

Aigrain, Rene. *Religious Music*. London: Sands & Co., n.d.

Albright, Raymond W. *Focus on Infinity: A Life of Phillips Brooks*. New York: Macmillan, 1961.

Bailey, Albert Edward. *The Gospel in Hymns*. New York: Charles Scribner's Sons, 1950.

Battiscombe, Georgina. *Christina Rossetti: A Divided Life*. New York: Holt, Rinehart and Winston, 1981.

Bell, Mackenzie. *Christina Rossetti*. London: Hurst and Blackett, 1898.

Bence, Evelyn. *Spiritual Moments with the Great Hymns*. Grand Rapids, Mich.: Zondervan Publishing House, 1997.

Benson, John Allanson. *Handel's Messiah*. London: Reeves, 1897.

Benson, Louis F. *The English Hymn*. Richmond, Va.: John Knox Press, 1962.

Berger, Melvin. *Guide to Choral Masterpieces*. New York: Doubleday Anchor Books, 1993.

Berlioz, Hector. *Memoirs*. New York: Alfred A. Knopf, Inc., 1932.

Bodine, William Budd. *Some Hymns and Hymn Writers*. Philadelphia: The John C. Winston Co., 1907.

Bonner, Clint. *A Hymn Is Born*. Nashville: Broadman Press, 1959.

Bradley, Ian, ed. *The Penguin Book of Carols*. London: Penguin Books, 1999.

Britt, Dom Matthew, ed. *The Hymns of the Breviary and Missal*. New York: Benziger Brothers, Inc., 1948.

Brown, Theron, and Hezekiah Butterworth. *The Story of the Hymns and Tunes*. New York: American Tract Society, 1907.

Chappell, Paul. *Music and Worship in the Anglican Church*. London: The Faith Press, 1968.

Christ-Janer, Albert, et al. *American Hymns Old and New*. New York: Columbia University Press, 1980.

Clark, Elmer T. *Charles Wesley: The Singer of the Evangelical Revival*. Nashville: The Upper Room, 1957.

Clark, W. K. Lowther. *A Hundred Years of Hymns, Ancient and Modern*. London: Clowes, 1961.

Colquttoun, Frank. *Hymns That Live*. Downers Grove, Ill.: InterVarsity Press, 1980.

Crews, C. Daniel. *Johann Friedrich Peter and His Times*. Winston Salem, N.C.: Moravian Music Foundation, 1990.

Cushman, Joseph D., Jr. *A Goodly Heritage: The Episcopal Church in Florida, 1821–1892.* Gainesville, Fla.: University of Florida Press, 1965.

Dallimore, Arnold A. *A Heart Set Free: The Life of Charles Wesley.* Wheaton, Ill.: Crossway Books, 1988.

Daves, Michael. *Famous Hymns and Their Writers.* Westwood, N.J.: Fleming H. Revell Company, 1962.

Davis, Paul. *Isaac Watts: His Life and Works.* New York: Dryden, 1943.

Dearmer, Percy, et al. *The Oxford Book of Carols.* London: Oxford University Press, 1928.

Dickinson, Edward. *Music in the History of the Western Church.* New York: Charles Scribner's Sons, 1953.

Donahoe, Daniel Joseph. *Early Christian Hymns.* New York: The Grafton Press, 1908.

Douglas, Winfred. *Church Music in History and Practice.* New York: Charles Scribner's Sons, 1937.

Duffield, Samuel Willoughby. *The Latin Hymn-Writers and Their Hymns.* New York: Funk and Wagnalls, 1889.

Duncan, Edmondstoune. *The Story of the Carol.* New York: Scribners, 1911.

Dunstan, Alan. *These Are the Hymns.* London: SPCK, 1973.

Ellinwood, Leonard. *The History of American Church Music.* New York: Da Capo Press, 1970.

Emurian, Ernest K. *Stories of Christmas Carols.* Boston: W. A. Wilde Company, 1967.

———. *Stories of Yuletide.* Natick, Mass.: W. A. Wilde Company, 1960.

Everett, Grace M. *Hymn Treasures.* Cincinnati: Jennings and Graham, 1905.

Fellerer, Karl Gustav. *The History of Catholic Church Music.* Baltimore, Md.: Helicon Press, 1961.

Foss, Hubert. *Ralph Vaughan Williams.* New York: Oxford University Press, 1950.

Fountain, David. *Isaac Watts Remembered.* Worthing, England: Henry E. Walter, Ltd., 1974.

Fox, Adam. *English Hymns and Hymn Makers.* London: Collins, 1947.

Gurlitt, Wilibald. *Johann Sebastian Bach: The Master and His Work.* St. Louis: Concordia, 1957.

Harvey, Peter. *Glory, Laud and Honour: Favourite Hymns and Their Stories.* London: SPCK, 1996.

Harvey, Robert. *Best-Loved Hymn Stories.* Grand Rapids: Zondervan, 1963.

Hewitt, Theodore Brown. *Paul Gerhardt as a Hymn Writer and His Influence on English Hymnody.* New Haven, Conn.: Yale University Press, 1918.

Hume, Paul. *Catholic Church Music.* New York: Dodd, Mead & Company, 1956.

Hutchings, Arthur. *Church Music in the Nineteenth Century.* London: Herbert Jenkins, 1967.

The Hymnal 1940 Companion. New York: The Church Pension Fund, 1949.

Idle, Christopher. *Stories of Our Favorite Hymns.* Grand Rapids: Eerdmans, 1980.

Jackson, George Pullen. *White Spirituals in the Southern Uplands.* Chapel Hill, N.C.: University of North Carolina Press, 1933.

Jacobs, Arthur, ed. *Choral Music.* Baltimore, Md.: Penguin Books, 1963.

Jefferson, H. A. L. *Hymns in Christian Worship.* New York: Macmillan, 1950.

Johnson, James Weldon and J. Rosamund. *The Books of American Negro Spirituals.* New York: Da Capo Press, 1954.

Jones, Francis Arthur. *Famous Hymns and Their Authors.* London: Hodder and Stoughton, 1902.

Julian, John. *A Dictionary of Hymnology.* London: John Murray, 1907.

Kavanaugh, Patrick. *The Music of Angels.* Chicago: Loyola Press, 1999.

———. *The Spiritual Lives of Great Composers.* Nashville: Sparrow Press, 1992.

Keyte, Hugh and Andrew Parrott, eds. *The Shorter New Oxford Book of Carols.* New York: Oxford University Press, 1993.

Konkle, Wilbur. *Living Hymn Stories.* Minneapolis: Bethany, 1971.

Lang, Paul Henry. *George Frideric Handel.* New York: W. W. Norton & Company, 1966.

Larsen, Jens Peter. *Handel's Messiah.* New York: W. W. Norton & Company, 1972.

Liderbach, Daniel. *Christ in the Early Christian Hymns.* New York: Paulist Press, 1998.

Lightwood, James Thomas. *The Music of the Methodist Hymn Book.* London: Epworth Press, 1935.

Limmer-Sheppard, W. J. *Great Hymns and Their Stories.* London: Epworth Press, 1950.

Long, Kenneth. *The Music of the English Church.* London: Hodder and Stoughton, 1991.

Lough, A. G. *The Influence of John Mason Neale.* London: SPCK, 1962.

———. *John Mason Neale—Priest Extraordinary.* Oxford, England: Bocardo Church Army Press Ltd., 1976.

Lovell, E. W. *A Green Hill Far Away.* Derry, Northern Ireland: Friends of St. Columb's Cathedral, 1994.

Mable, Norman. *Popular Hymns and Their Writers.* London: Independent Press, 1944.

Manning, Bernard C. *The Hymns of Wesley and Watts.* London: Epworth, 1942.

Marek, George R. *Gentle Genius: The Story of Felix Mendelssohn.* New York: Funk & Wagnalls, 1972.

McGuckin, John Anthony, translator. *At the Lighting of the Lamps: Hymns of the Ancient Church.* Oxford, England: SLG Press, 1995.

Menendez, Albert J. and Shirley C. *Christmas Songs Made in America: Favorite Holiday Melodies and the Stories of Their Origins.* Nashville: Cumberland House, 1999.

Moser, Hans Joachim. *Heinrich Schutz: His Life and Work.* St. Louis: Concordia, 1959.

Myers, Robert Manson. *Handel's Messiah: A Touchstone of Taste*. New York: Octagon Books, 1971.

Nettle, Reginald. *Christmas and Its Carols*. London: Faith Press, 1960.

Northcott, Cecil. *Hymns We Love*. Philadelphia: Westminster Press, 1955.

Packer, Lona Mosk. *Christina Rossetti*. Cambridge: Cambridge University Press, 1963.

Parry, Kenneth L. *Christian Hymns*. London: SCM Press, Ltd., 1956.

Patterson, Annie W. *The Story of Oratorio*. New York: Charles Scribner's Sons, 1915.

Pauli, Hertha. *Handel and the Messiah Story*. New York: Meredith, 1968.

———. *Silent Night: The Story of a Song*. New York: Alfred A. Knopf, 1943.

Pennington, Edgar Legare. *Soldier and Servant: John Freeman Young, Second Bishop of Florida*. Hartford, Conn.: Church Missions Publishing Company, 1939.

Peters, Erskine. *Lyrics of the Afro-American Spiritual*. Westport, Conn.: Greenwood Press, 1993.

Phillips, Charles Stanley. *Hymnody Past and Present*. London: SPCK, 1937.

Price, Carl. *One Hundred and One Hymn Stories*. Nashville: Abingdon, 1923.

Rainbow, Bernard. *The Choral Revival in the Anglican Church, 1839–1872*. New York: Oxford University Press, 1970.

Reynolds, William J. *Christ and the Carols*. Nashville: Broadman Press, 1967.

———. *Hymns of Our Faith*. Nashville: Broadman, 1964.

Richards, Katharine L. *How Christmas Came to the Sunday Schools*. New York: Dodd, Mead, and Company, 1934.

Riedel, Johannes. *The Lutheran Chorale*. Minneapolis: Augsburg Publishing House, 1967.

Robertson, Alec. *Christian Music*. New York: Hawthorn Books, 1961.

Roth, Nancy. *Awake, My Soul!* New York: Church Publishing Incorporated, 1999.

Routley, Erik. *The English Carol*. London: Herbert Jenkins, 1958.

———. *The Music of Catholic Hymnody*. London: Independent Press, 1957.

———. *A Short History of English Church Music*. Carol Stream, Ill.: Hope Publishing Company, 1997.

Rutler, George William. *Brightest and Best: Stories of Hymns*. San Francisco: Ignatius Press, 1998.

Ryden, Ernest Edwin. *The Story of Christian Hymnody*. Philadelphia, Pa.: Fortress Press, 1959.

Sandars, Mary F. *Christina Rossetti*. London: Hutchinson, 1930.

Scholes, Percy A., ed. *The Oxford Companion to Music*. New York: Oxford University Press, 1970.

Seeger, Ruth Crawford. *American Folk Songs for Christmas*. New York: Doubleday, 1953.

Simon, Henry W., ed. *A Treasury of Christmas Songs and Carols*. Boston: Houghton Mifflin, 1973.

Smith, H. Augustine. *Lyric Religion: The Romance of Immortal Hymns*. New York: Fleming H. Revell Company, 1931.

Squire, Russel N. *Church Music*. St. Louis: Bethany Press, 1962.

Stevenson, Robert. *Protestant Church Music in America*. New York: Norton, 1970.

Stuart, D. M. *Christina Rossetti*. London: Macmillan, 1930.

Studwell, William E. *The Christmas Carol Reader*. New York: Haworth Press, Inc., 1995.

––––––. *Christmas Carols: A Reference Guide*. New York: Garland Publishing, Inc., 1985.

––––––, and Dorothy E. Jones. *Publishing Glad Tidings: Essays on Christmas Music*. New York: Haworth Press, Inc., 1998.

Sweet, Charles F. *A Champion of the Cross: The Life of John Henry Hopkins*. New York: James Pott and Co., 1894.

Terry, Richard. *Catholic Church Music*. London: Greening & Co., Ltd., 1907.

Towle, Eleanor A. *John Mason Neale: A Memoir*. New York: Longmans, Green, and Co., 1906.

Turnbull, Robert. *Musical Genius and Religion*. London: Elkin Matthews, 1907.

Wallace, Valerie. *Mrs. Alexander: A Life of the Hymn-Writer*. Dublin: The Lilliput Press, 1995.

Walpole, A. S., and A. J. Mason, eds. *Early Latin Hymns*. London: Cambridge University Press, 1922.

Warren, Gwendolin Sims. *Ev'ry Time I Feel the Spirit*. New York: Henry Holt, 1997.

Weiser, Francis X. *The Christmas Book*. New York: Harcourt, Brace and Company, 1952.

––––––. *Handbook of Christian Feasts and Customs*. New York: Harcourt, Brace and Company, 1958.

Wernecke, Herbert. *Christmas Songs and Their Stories*. Philadelphia, Pa.: Westminster Press, 1957.

Young, John Freeman. *Great Hymns of the Church*. New York: James Pott and Co., 1887.

Young, Percy M. *The Choral Tradition*. New York. W. W. Norton & Company, Inc., 1971.

––––––. *Handel*. London: J. M. Dent, 1975

INDEX